MW01516929

beaut utes 3

'the uteman'
allan m. nixon

PENGUIN BOOKS

Penguin Books Australia Ltd
487 Maroondah Highway, PO Box 257
Ringwood, Victoria 3134, Australia
Penguin Books Ltd
Harmondsworth, Middlesex, England
Penguin Putnam Inc.
375 Hudson Street, New York, New York 10014, USA
Penguin Books Canada Limited
10 Alcorn Avenue, Toronto, Ontario, Canada M4V 3B2
Penguin Books (NZ) Ltd
Cnr Rosedale and Airborne Roads, Albany, Auckland, New Zealand
Penguin Books (South Africa) (Pty) Ltd
24 Sturdee Avenue, Rosebank, Johannesburg 2196, South Africa
Penguin Books India (P) Ltd
11, Community Centre, Panchsheel Park, New Delhi 110 017, India

First published by Penguin Books Australia 2001

1 3 5 7 9 10 8 6 4 2

Copyright © Allan M. Nixon 2001

The moral right of the author has been asserted

All rights reserved. Without limiting the rights under copyright
reserved above, no part of this publication may be reproduced,
stored in or introduced into a retrieval system, or transmitted, in
any form or by any means (electronic, mechanical, photocopying,
recording or otherwise), without the prior written permission of both
the copyright owner and the above publisher of this book.

Book design by Geoff Hocking
Co-design by Allan M. Nixon
Cover photograph by Colin Barr
Printed and bound by
Bookbuilders, China

National Library of Australia
Cataloguing-in-Publication data:

Nixon, Allan M., 1951– .
Beaut utes 3: the uteman.
ISBN 0 14 100778 8.
1. Motor vehicles – Australia – History.
2. Trucks – Australia – History.
3. Trucks – Australia – Anecdotes I.
Title.

629.223

www.penguin.com.au

Dedicated to my parents
Lorna & Roy Nixon
Who understand the meaning of a writer's life.
Thanks for the support.

And a special thanks to
HENRY LAWSON (1867–1922)
'The first articulate voice of Australia.'

He's always been my guiding source of inspiration.
May he live on in the heart and soul of Australia —
forever.

'When I Get My Wheels' & 'King of the Road'
(words & music Adam Brand) © Universal Music
Publishing Pty Ltd. Reproduced by kind permission
of Universal Music Publishing Pty Ltd.

Contents

Introduction

UTES:
A New Direction

WHEN THE ORIGINAL *BEAUT UTES* BOOK came out in 1998, the ute scene was just beginning to be noticed and someone said to me a book on utes wouldn't work. Well, it became a bestseller, as did the sequel *More Beaut Utes*. Not only that, but two other authors have also published their own ute books. And there's more coming.

When researching the first book women commented to me on how they got a hard time if they owned a ute. Now there are many women owners and they can hold their own with any bloke when it comes to loving their utes. Times have changed quickly when it comes to utes.

When the first *Beaut Utes 2000 Calendar* came out, little did we realise that soon you would be able to buy any number of ute calendars all over Australia. Then came the first CD – *Ute Drivin' Man*, with 14 original songs all about the utes of Australia.

Ute shows have exploded around Australia; almost every country town has their own now. We've had Dog 'n Ute Queues, Ute Musters and now it's Ford-v-Holden ute racing. Almost every magazine and newspaper features major stories concerning utes. The original Uteman website, started in 1998, was on its own; now there are many great sites dedicated to the ute.

Everyone, it seems, loves the ute. It has come of age. Thousands of us ute lovers around Australia already knew what a great vehicle the ute is. Now it is even trendy in the city to own a ute and ute sales have never been higher.

Ford AU ute sales have broken every record; now Holden VU are out to do the same and it seems as if our two major suppliers have different directions.

General Motors Holden is after the youth market with the beaut VU; and the UTEster, a convertible ute, high-tech with low profile tyres. Whilst they have the sleek and sexy record-breaking XR8 V8 ute, Ford seems to be heading down the tradesmen track and the four-wheel drive, off-road route. (That is my own personal opinion; perhaps Ford and Holden would not agree.)

Whatever they and other manufacturers choose, there is no doubt that everyone is onto the ute market, overseas companies also – VW, Chev, Honda, Toyota and other manufacturers are all looking at releasing various interpretations of the ute. Some are the real thing, others are mere toys. Some companies are simply jumping onto the bandwagon. Or should we say, the utewagon?

Many say there are only two real utes – Ford and Holden. Tell that to Toyota, Nissan, Landrover and a multitude of other people who love their type of ute.

If it has a rear tray, it'll do me!

I'm just glad to be a small part of it all.

UTE MAN

A New Direction

SINCE 1998, I HAVE HAD THE PLEASURE OF travelling many parts of Australia judging ute shows, writing articles for a magazine and researching books, including this one. I would have to say, in doing so, I have met some of the greatest people you could ever wish to meet and many are in this book.

There is despair in rural Australia; I have seen many communities change and those changes have meant that the 'bush' will never be the same. Some of the once thriving towns are struggling; many shops now lie empty and will probably never reopen. But I have also seen that great Aussie bush spirit come alive and communities, in order to survive, have come together like never before. Many areas are showing the way; they have taken on change and hit it fair and square between the eyes, showing that the get-up-and-go attitude is still alive.

I adore this land and the more I travel Australia, the more I love it. I am glad to share with readers some of the characters and landscape that this country is famous for. The people in this book are just a sample of what this country is all about – diversity, individuality, humour, rugged strength and refined talent. These are some great Australians from all sorts of backgrounds. It is an honour to bring you a glimpse of their lives and of their utes.

These are just some of the ute drivers of Australia:

May their travels through life always be on smooth roads.

The Four Elements of The Ute

THEY SAY EVERYTHING IS MADE UP OF the four elements - Earth, Wind, Fire and Water. Well, in the case of utes, it is the earth beneath the wheels when you are on a dusty track, the wind in your face when you've smashed the windscreen, it's the water in the radiator when she's boiling, and it's the fire in your belly when you start up that V8. And that's just the start.

EARTH -

- Dust in ya face, mate.
- Circleworking the paddock.
- Soil in the back to make the garden grow.
- Red dust of the Outback.
- And when the rains come - she's the mud that sticks you in a bog.

WIND -

- Dog in the back, wind in the gob.
- Air-conditioner blowing hard.
- Head wind slowing you down.
- Tail wind heading for home.

FIRE -

- Sun beating down.
- Frying eggs on a red-hot motor.
- Blow out – burning rubber.
- Campfire burning, billy on the boil, and swags laid out.

WATER -

- Leaking rain through the cracks in the old HJ.
- Sweat pouring off your face on a hot summer day.
- None left in the radiator and your blood will boil.
- Praying for rain in a dry bush land.

Ute drivers all over Australia could add their own great list of battling the four elements.

I'd love to hear yours, so why not email me on uteman@origin.net.au or drop me a line at P.O.Box 46, North Essendon, Victoria, 3041.

Keep on Uteing!

Allan M. Nixon
The Uteman
Anzac Day, 25 April 2001

And please remember what The Uteman says:

- *Tomato sauce on fried rice really is quite nice.*
- *Henry Lawson was, and is, a hero for Australia.*
- *As long as there is society – thank God, there'll always be republicans!*
- *Who knows if Ned Kelly's helmet fitted or not?*
- *If you get a dog, don't get a cross-bred that is half 'in the ute' and half 'home and away'.*
- *Close the bloody gate if that's the way you found it!*
- *Smile because stress might blow your head off.*
- *Get a life - get a ute!*
- *May the ring spanner you require always be in the toolbox.*

A-Model $35 Buckboard

When he starts it up it sounds like a Massey Ferguson tractor on steroids.

SOUNDS LIKE 'DAD AND DAVE' OR ONE of 'The Beverly Hillbillies' should drive this ute. But Tony Berry is the proud owner of this great 1928 Ford A-Model Buckboard ute.

'I've driven it like hell and badly treated it. It's a ridiculous spectacle, but I fell in love with it and will never sell it.'

Tony is a man of my own thinking. He too believes that old vehicles have great worth simply being in their original condition, and NOT being restored is sometimes more exciting than having a better-than-new vehicle.

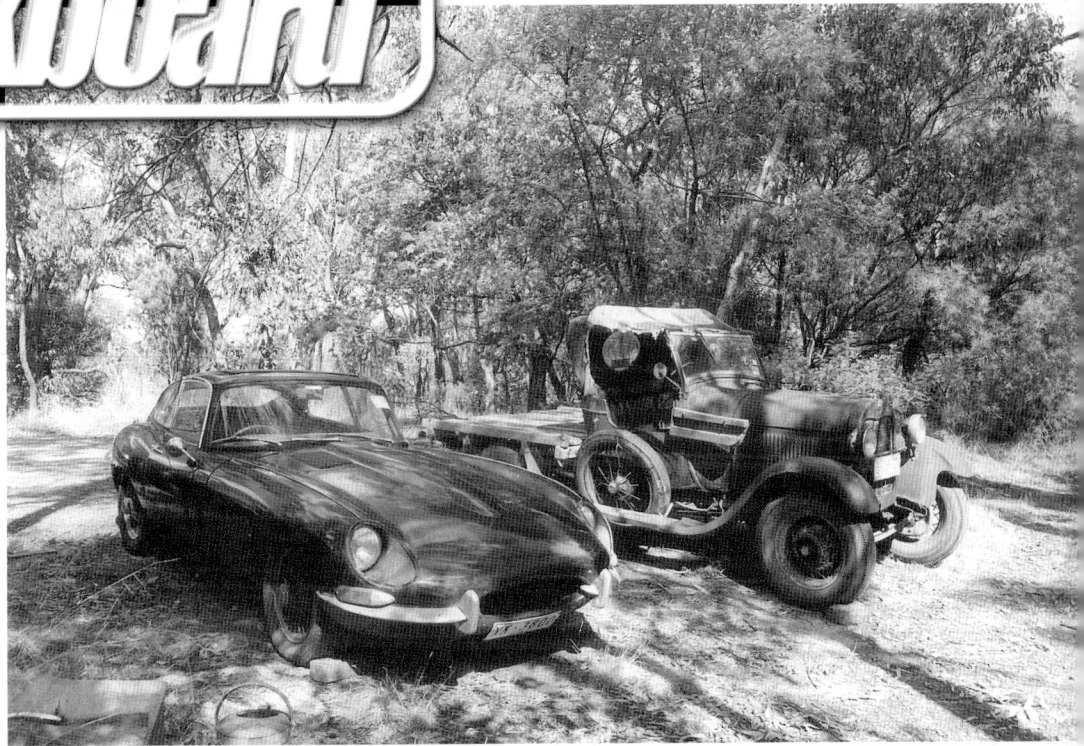

There is something very special about finding a great old vehicle, all covered in dust, in a shed and seeing it return to a driveable condition without having to get out the paint spray. I love looking at something very old and learning all about its great history. I have owned restored and unrestored vehicles; both are great. Some deserve nothing less than the best spent on them, but equally, some deserve to have their original beauty retained.

Read Ray Stevens' story *[see Exquisite! Dodge and a Holden page 54]* and tell me I should restore the 1925 Dodge. For me it would be taking away much of its beauty - it would become just another restored ute. Its history of hard work, weathering the elements and more is all there in its originality. I love it. Tony has a similar feeling for his ute.

Tony Berry's passion for his ute is evident. He bought it at a clearing sale at an old property. He bid $25 for it but two old fencers bid him up for the fun of it, so he had to pay $35. It had a rolling chassis. Two weeks later he found another in an old shed and paid $40 for it.

'It was a good vehicle but was a bit of an oil burner; it used about a quarter of

a pint of oil to travel 15 kilometres. But I just fell in love with it. I've rebuilt the engine and gearbox and spent about $1200 on it. I bought it in 1982. Originally, I drove it unregistered as a shooting ute.'

The ute is a bit of a bitzer. The rear tub was found in an old goldmine and welded straight on. The left door kept falling off. The windscreen is from a pre-war MG. It has English headlights, an Alfa Romeo fuel filter, a Holden alternator. The seat is from a 403 Peugeot, the wipers are from a cabin cruiser, it has no muffler ('waste of time on the side valve motor') and the exhaust is a tailshaft from an FJ Holden ('they don't wear out'). It has a Ford 10 distributor that has an automatic advance and retard, the front wheels are from a 34 Ford and the rear ones have been cut down from 21-inch to 16-inch and welded onto Peugeot rims. The rest is all pure A-Model Ford. It is still registered.

Tony says it is so easy to work on – a spanner and screwdriver and you can practically rebuild it. It had 54 000 miles on it when he bought it, but he has no idea what it's done now.

'I put it in a car and ute show where Peter Brock was the judge and we got talking about chassis flex. He was really interested – but he didn't bloody give the ute first prize.

'The original canvas hood used to get blown off if something like a bloody Kenworth truck drove by. So I made a hood from fibreglass, then covered it with the original canvas and plastered 1932s *Truth* and *Argus* newspapers on the inside of the roof. If you break down, at least you have some interesting reading.

'I used it for work every day for about 10 years. As a bricklayer it has been loaded - God, it has been loaded. But it was good for my business. I was offered a lot from a well-known bloke who wanted it because of its condition. I've had many offers.

'It has never been garaged, always left in the open. It sat in a paddock and was not used for 12 months at one stage.

'I've driven it to the Tamworth Country Music Festival five times and driven in the cavalcade parade each time. Whenever I drive to Tamworth the same cops pull me up and check it over and also a lot of businesses in small towns along the way know

the ute. I've taken it to Queensland a couple of times and to Fraser Island, Renmark, Mildura and to the Phillip Island Classic Car races. It's very strong and when I knew I could get new parts for it easily, I thought, "Why not?" It always goes well when it's warm.'

Tony's sense of humour is evident when he talks of the ute too. **'If I get depressed, I just jump in it and go for a** burn. If I get real depressed I throw in a cup of kerosene and go into the city and really cheese people off - they can smell it coming. Actually, it runs quite well on kerosene, but it's too dear now. I have a low-line canopy for it - a galvanised water tank cut in half and I throw it on the back. I also protect it with fish oil all over it. Actually, tuna oil and fish guts pushed into the rust holes is great. It goes off and it is the best of natural glues.'

Tony Berry has had an interesting 54 years. He grew up living on the semi-rural fringe, next door to one of Bill's Circus' winter grounds. He has fond memories of vehicles, similar to his present A-model, that were used by the local orchardists at the time.

In 1968 Tony was called up to do national service and spent 12 months in Vietnam as a driver of armoured personnel carriers in the Third Cavalry Regiment, transporting troops into battle or rescuing them from ambush. He lost four mates in battle and was always in the thick of it. Like many of the vets, he lived on the adrenalin addiction of war - a life of continual stress, killing, mayhem and fear.

Then he returned home to a country ostracising those who had served their country. He was a good Christian and when he returned he joined in on two moratorium marches to ban the war. Like many veterans he found it hard to return to a normal life.

'I hit the road, became an itinerant - hitching and picking fruit and doing all sorts of jobs. Later I returned to study engineering for two or three years but dropped out and went fishing as a deckhand on a cray boat, and then later I did shark fishing off Bermagui. I had also trained as a diver in the military but didn't go ahead with it in civilian life. Then bricklaying seemed the closest thing to a free life for me, so I spent the next 20 years in the building trade.'

Tony has a daughter, Poppy, who works for the RSL in hospitality management, and a stepdaughter, Sunny, who works as an activities officer at a university.

'I bought this bush block in about 1970, and arrived here to live in a tent with a lounge suite and a kero fridge.'

Around the block today is an absolute plethora of stuff. He loves anything old and hates wastage. At the moment his daily vehicle is an E-type Jaguar. Around the property there is an Austin 7 paddock car, a Holden HQ ('rust bucket with original motor but no floor') and six dead Mercedes Benz. There is also a 1922 Vauxhall in one shed. He used to have an FX ute, but it was more rust than ute.

'There are stacks of other basket cases around here also,' he says.

There are also numerous boats and in one huge shed there is a 40-foot, steel-hulled boat that Tony is building. Tony sells nothing unless he really has to and that is rare. He would much rather use things as he needs them.

He is a keen sailor having sailed from Sydney to Hobart, through Bass Strait, up and down the Queensland coast, all around the Mediterranean, through the canals of France, and in the North Sea.

Tony Berry is no fool and his library shows that he is well read – clearly an intelligent man. He says he is a lateral thinker and has always been practical. Just looking around you can see he is a very creative person and he has always liked old stuff. His mum, who is 85 and still plays the church organ, cooked on a wood stove until a few years back. 'Her father was a salesman for Floods, and she was always a bit of a petrol head too.'

Tony was always into English cars, but then he found that the American cars were made of very good materials - the quality of Ford vehicles impressed him. Now he reckons that some of those old English cars look like they were made by a committee of blacksmiths!

The strength of his ute impresses him as he says he 'always was flaying it to death, a lot of the time, sideways.'

'Tony is slightly feral, bent, artistic, anal retentive, messy and a slob, but he is loving most of the time,' says Leslie Avril, his girlfriend of 10 years.

He describes her as 'having more balls than a Tattslotto machine, feisty and fun, exuberant and joyful, grumpy and hibernating in a burrow.'

It's obvious that they are soul mates but also independent souls at the same time – a lot of fun. When she pulled up in her nice Mercedes, I wondered: what does Avril think of the ute?

'Oh, it's a national treasure. When I first saw it, I got a bit of a shock and was a bit embarrassed driving around in it. It's definitely got personality - it's great fun sitting on the back of it and singing.' Avril really likes the ute. Tony reckons ladies like the vibration that comes through the seat.

'I've never had sex in it,' says Avril with a great laugh. 'I have', says Tony. 'I remember getting a head job as I drove along in it.' He relates all about it but we can't repeat any more here.

Avril too has had a ute - a silver Ford XY with a white canopy and V8. 'Boy, that went,' she recalls. But her fondest memories

are of her purple HQ panel van that she bought when she was 18. It had purple curtains and purple carpet. Her father was not impressed. She said she wanted it to carry her music equipment around in.

Avril grew up in a musical family. Her father was John Bowker – a singer – and her mother, Adele Jarrett – a dancer. Both were in theatre productions with J.C. Williamson until 1958 in Australia and New Zealand. They played in *Pyjama Game*, *Can Can* and many other productions.

Avril is a talented singer and musician. She learned classical piano, ballet, dancing and singing. She joined a band and has released three country music CDs. She is a regular performer at the Tamworth Country Music Festival each year. You can read all about her career at her website – www.leslieavril.com

Tony is now retired and on a military pension, but still does some creative work around his property. He is currently building a two-storey studio for Avril.

And so our time had come to an end. It was great spending time with these two creative and interesting people. We had enjoyed some laughs and some cups of tea, and yarned about the good things of life. Tony now very much appreciates his lifestyle in a peaceful and natural environment.

If ever he has a clearing sale, I'll be there buying it by the ute load. He has some great junk, and good stuff it is too.

Just remember, Tony, there is always room for the A-Model Buckboard in my National Beaut Utes Museum.

Adam Brand *Dirt Track* Cowboy

'When I get my wheels,
    I'm gonna ride right by,

You can eat my dust,
    and try to keep up

Man, I'd like to see you try,

I'll have my pedal to the metal,
    my claw to the floor

As I disappear out of sight,

When I get my wheels,
    I won't even wave goodbye.' [1]

WHEN HE LEFT PERTH AND HEADED EAST
to become a country singer, Adam had
loaded his XF Falcon ute with all his possessions – bulging suitcases and guitars.

'The ute was chock-a-block,' Adam
recalls. He sold everything and crossed the
Nullarbor with hope and talent in his
heart. Times were tough; his only real
contact was Graham Thompson, who would
later become Adam's manager. There was
no CD and no recording contract. But he

did have some songs and a commitment to success.

'When I arrived in Sydney, Graham helped me unpack the ute. It was a cold winter and the ute didn't have any anti-freeze in it. One morning I spent three hours with a little blow heater trying to get the thing to work.'

Finally, Adam's first single *King of the Road* came out on 13 July 1997 as an independent single, and the ute was loaded up again with boxes of the CD.

A self-confessed revhead from way back, the song shows his interest in utes.

**'Joey had a ute built in '74
Had a 350 Chevvie and a four
on the floor
Had chrome wire wheels
And a customised back
He could run the quarter mile
in under ten flat'.** [2]

Adam hit the road and went on a tour throughout New South Wales. He simply walked into record shops and country radio stations and gave them a CD saying

'G'day, my name is Adam Brand and this is my new CD.' He gave away about 200 CDs, just so he could introduce himself.

His travels took his ute from Sydney to Brisbane and to places like Tamworth, Moree, Inverell, Muswellbrook, Tenterfield, Lismore and Coff's Harbour. A later trip took him out to Bourke, Dubbo, Wagga, Griffith, and onto places like Cowra, Nowra, Bateman's Bay, and even through Victoria's far East Gippsland to Bairnsdale.

In January 1997, Adam was busking in the streets of Tamworth. He finally got a recording deal and his single *Last Man Standing* saw him on the road again. All up, he thinks he travelled about 20 000 kilometres doing promotion work around the countryside. On 13 July 1998, exactly 12 months to the day after his first single, his first album – *The Blue Album* – came out.

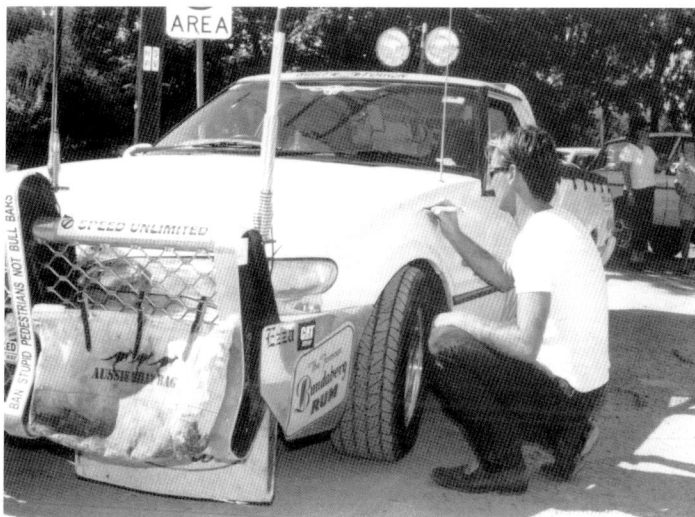

In January 1999, he was back in Tamworth – this time to collect three Golden Guitar Awards. In January 2000, he collected another Golden Guitar Award, and in January 2001 he stormed Tamworth and took out another three major Golden Guitar Awards. It was an emotional time for Adam. He was more surprised than anyone and acknowledged with due reverence that he had won in the same category as the great legends of the country music industry – Slim Dusty and Lee Kernaghan.

A total of seven Golden Guitar Awards in the last three years are great memories for his bookshelf, but out in the backyard is another: his trusty XF Falcon ute. **'She'll never be sold. She's a good old girl, we left Perth together and now she's a real keepsake.'**

As well as the XF Falcon ute, success has also brought him an XR8 ute, courtesy of a two-year deal with Ford.

At Tamworth on January 26, Adam Brand turned 31 years old. He spent days performing on stage, placing his hands into cement at the Hands of Fame ceremony, signing autographs, attending media interview after interview. On the Saturday, we loaded him into the back of the ute and drove him in the procession down the main street where he was met by adoring fans who were clapping and cheering, taking his photo and asking for autographs.

He ended up partying with Lee Kernaghan until 5.30 am, playing the piano and sharing a bottle of Wild Turkey, which was the prize for a bet on who would win. Adam just did not believe that he would. With little sleep, he was out on the rounds by 9.00 am on Sunday, swamped by the media for most of that day.

He has a new CD in the pipeline and his workload has just increased even more. This will be a huge year for Adam and his manager, Graham Thompson, co-owner of Compass Brothers.

And how does a bloke who has had such a huge and successful weekend wind down? Well, if you saw two XR8 utes heading in convoy from Tamworth to Sydney, it was Adam and I. He wanted to take my wife, Janette, and I to the Paramatta Speedway to see the dirt track cowboys do their thing. He received a huge ovation when he was introduced to the crowd, as he is well known at all the racetracks. He is their number one revhead and supporter and he has done much for their sport. His song *Dirt Track Cowboys* was a huge success.

A generous and giving man, people have warmed to the good looking young bloke who has a thirst for success but is only too willing to give of his time and more. He has performed at over 60 primary schools

The Four Elements of The Ute

THEY SAY EVERYTHING IS MADE UP OF the four elements - Earth, Wind, Fire and Water. Well, in the case of utes, it is the earth beneath the wheels when you are on a dusty track, the wind in your face when you've smashed the windscreen, it's the water in the radiator when she's boiling, and it's the fire in your belly when you start up that V8. And that's just the start.

EARTH -

- Dust in ya face, mate.
- Circleworking the paddock.
- Soil in the back to make the garden grow.
- Red dust of the Outback.
- And when the rains come - she's the mud that sticks you in a bog.

WIND -

- Dog in the back, wind in the gob.
- Air-conditioner blowing hard.
- Head wind slowing you down.
- Tail wind heading for home.

FIRE -

- Sun beating down.
- Frying eggs on a red-hot motor.
- Blow out - burning rubber.
- Campfire burning, billy on the boil, and swags laid out.

WATER -

- Leaking rain through the cracks in the old HJ.
- Sweat pouring off your face on a hot summer day.
- None left in the radiator and your blood will boil.
- Praying for rain in a dry bush land.

Ute drivers all over Australia could add their own great list of battling the four elements.

I'd love to hear yours, so why not email me on uteman@origin.net.au or drop me a line at P.O.Box 46, North Essendon, Victoria, 3041.

Keep on Uteing!

Allan M. Nixon
The Uteman
Anzac Day, 25 April 2001

And please remember what The Uteman says:

- Tomato sauce on fried rice really is quite nice.
- Henry Lawson was, and is, a hero for Australia.
- As long as there is society - thank God, there'll always be republicans!
- Who knows if Ned Kelly's helmet fitted or not?
- If you get a dog, don't get a cross-bred that is half 'in the ute' and half 'home and away'.
- Close the bloody gate if that's the way you found it!
- Smile because stress might blow your head off.
- Get a life - get a ute!
- May the ring spanner you require always be in the toolbox.

A-Model $35 Buckboard

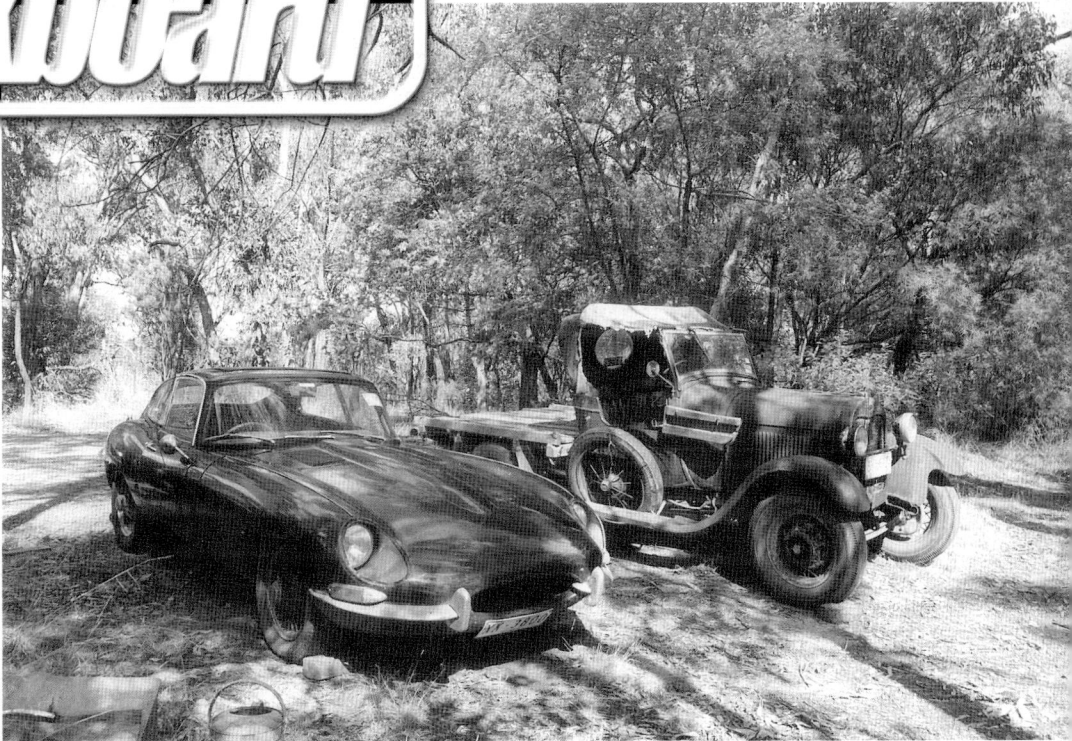

When he starts it up it sounds like a Massey Ferguson tractor on steroids.

SOUNDS LIKE 'DAD AND DAVE' OR ONE of 'The Beverly Hillbillies' should drive this ute. But Tony Berry is the proud owner of this great 1928 Ford A-Model Buckboard ute.

'I've driven it like hell and badly treated it. It's a ridiculous spectacle, but I fell in love with it and will never sell it.'

Tony is a man of my own thinking. He too believes that old vehicles have great worth simply being in their original condition, and NOT being restored is sometimes more exciting than having a better-than-new vehicle.

There is something very special about finding a great old vehicle, all covered in dust, in a shed and seeing it return to a driveable condition without having to get out the paint spray. I love looking at something very old and learning all about its great history. I have owned restored and unrestored vehicles; both are great. Some deserve nothing less than the best spent on them, but equally, some deserve to have their original beauty retained.

Read Ray Stevens' story *[see Exquisite! Dodge and a Holden page 54]* and tell me I should restore the 1925 Dodge. For me it would be taking away much of its beauty - it would become just another restored ute. Its history of hard work, weathering the elements and more is all there in its originality. I love it. Tony has a similar feeling for his ute.

Tony Berry's passion for his ute is evident. He bought it at a clearing sale at an old property. He bid $25 for it but two old fencers bid him up for the fun of it, so he had to pay $35. It had a rolling chassis. Two weeks later he found another in an old shed and paid $40 for it.

'It was a good vehicle but was a bit of an oil burner; it used about a quarter of a pint of oil to travel 15 kilometres. But I just fell in love with it. I've rebuilt the engine and gearbox and spent about $1200 on it. I bought it in 1982. Originally, I drove it unregistered as a shooting ute.'

The ute is a bit of a bitzer. The rear tub was found in an old goldmine and welded straight on. The left door kept falling off. The windscreen is from a pre-war MG. It has English headlights, an Alfa Romeo fuel filter, a Holden alternator. The seat is from a 403 Peugeot, the wipers are from a cabin cruiser, it has no muffler ('waste of time on the side valve motor') and the exhaust is a tailshaft from an FJ Holden ('they don't wear out'). It has a Ford 10 distributor that has an automatic advance and retard, the front wheels are from a 34 Ford and the rear ones have been cut down from 21-inch to 16-inch and welded onto Peugeot rims. The rest is all pure A-Model Ford. It is still registered.

Tony says it is so easy to work on – a spanner and screwdriver and you can practically rebuild it. It had 54 000 miles on it when he bought it, but he has no idea what it's done now.

Allenby the Eccentric

'He used to run 100 miles a week - religiously.'

HE WAS A MARATHON RUNNER UNTIL HE was 48, when he blew up the valves in his heart. He used to spar with Jack Absalom who was a champion boxer. When he died at 71 years of age, he was still the Australian champion pole vaulter for the over 70s.

'He did everything full-bore and flat-out. He had a mad drive of determination. He always picked out the unusual and went for it. He was a fanatic for making things, and was the inventor of amazing contraptions. He invented pottery equipment, a seed potato cutter, mining equipment, steel boats and once he even built a helicopter.'

You soon get the impression that Allenby Stuchbery was not the usual sort of bloke, and I'd have to say his son Ray, better known as Blue the Bush Larrikin, has inherited some of his father's drive. *[Read Blue's story in More Beaut Utes and also an update here on page 124.]*

Allenby left home at 14 and joined the railways at the Melbourne workshops where he learnt his trade of boilermaking. During the war years he was on the Oodnadatta Track. He married in Port Augusta.

'It was there that he bought the 1934 Ford roadster ute. I still remember it from my young years. It was painted burgundy and black with chrome wheels. Registration number: HM554,' says Blue proudly. 'It was later made into a "woody". He met Mum (Margaret) who was working in a store at the time. She had worked on stations and her father was a rouseabout around Wilcannia, Quorn and all through the Outback. Mum's still alive and lives nearby.'

After the war the Stuchberys moved to Bendigo where Allenby got a job at the ordinance factory. He remained there for

30 odd years as an A grade foreman boilermaker.

He was on long service leave and going around Australia when he fell in love with White Cliffs in outback New South Wales. He bought a 99-year lease frontage on Turley's Hill for a 'dugout' in the opal digging town.

In 1974 he commenced enlarging the tunnels in the side of the hill, then bought the lease next door for $300 and joined the two into one large underground home and art gallery. He called it 'Eagle's Nest' after two eagles that always flew around that spot. He was full of ideas.

It is now 300 feet from the front door to the back door, built on three levels, with a 360-degree observation deck on top, with huge glass windows. That room alone is 16 squares!

Allenby retired at 51 due to ill health. He was a keen supporter of anything sporting, and had been all his life. There was no way he could sit still. He took on a new interest - pottery. Two of his sons had already shown their talent in this area. Ray is a pottery teacher and David is a senior lecturer in ceramics. *[See his story here also on page 124.]*

Members of the family have contributed many pieces to the art gallery in the dugout at White Cliffs. Mrs Stuchbery is also an artist and music runs in the family too. Allenby played the harmonica and was a great yodeller. The children also play a variety of instruments.

The original dugout was built of second-hand material that was mostly donated or recycled. He would load whatever he had and head off from Bendigo to White Cliffs in his little Datsun 1500 tray-top ute.

He bought the ute in 1978 from a Bendigo local. He had seen it advertised in a newspaper while lying in a hospital bed.

Allenby added the things he needed for work, such as a vice on the tray, then a crane for lifting. Often the crane lifted items that were so heavy, the front wheels lifted off the ground, so he made outriggers to go underneath to support the ute.

Welding machinery was mounted on the tray and generated by a pulley from the back wheel. Steel fabrication aids were added such as a folder, numerous bending devices, uprights to plait wire and to

It also gave him the chance to do the sculptures he loved to make in the Outback. **He'd call into a remote home- stead, see on old square dis- used water tank, ask the owner's permission and then do oxy-weld art with designs such as the Southern Cross stars in it. Then he'd leave. He always liked to leave some form of artwork behind in the Outback.** He also did pottery and called himself 'Jonnie Mulga'.

While on holidays at 'Eagle's Nest' dugout in White Cliffs, his grandson, Matthew, then eight, learnt to drive the ute. He'd go off in the ute and collect rocks for his grandfather and was paid $5 an hour.

create the shapes he required for his building. He was a welcome sight to many a property owner - a boilermaker by trade, he often did that much-needed welding.

'Dad was quite eccen- tric,' says daughter, Anne, with a laugh and son, Ray (Blue), dryly adds, 'Yeah, Dad didn't really know how to load the ute, so he'd throw two loads on it at once to be sure.'

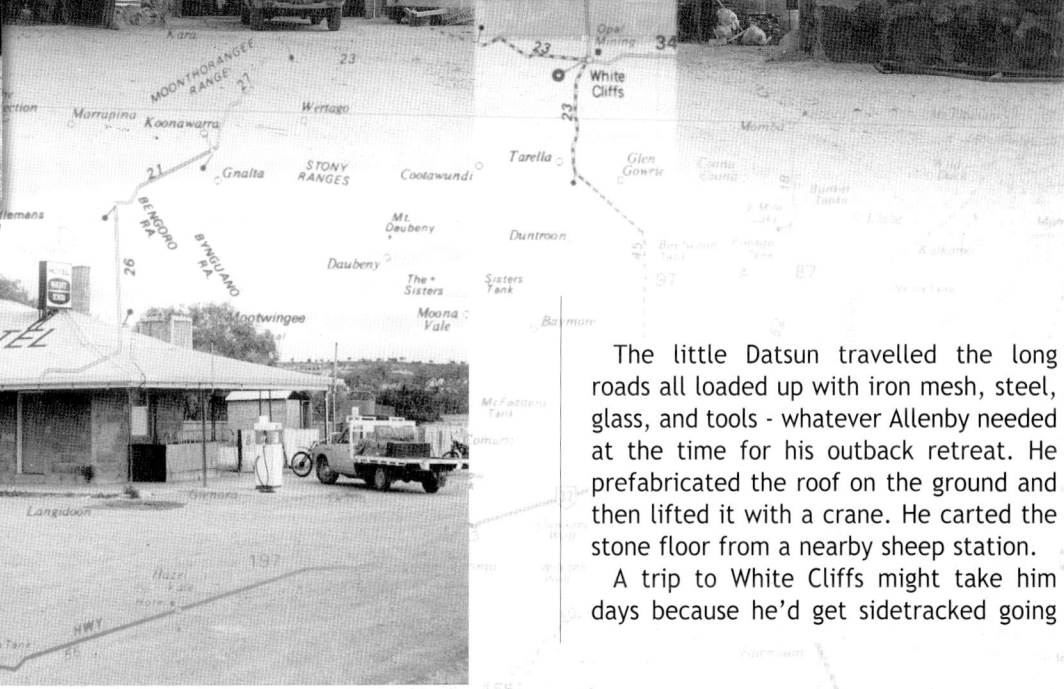

The little Datsun travelled the long roads all loaded up with iron mesh, steel, glass, and tools - whatever Allenby needed at the time for his outback retreat. He prefabricated the roof on the ground and then lifted it with a crane. He carted the stone floor from a nearby sheep station.

A trip to White Cliffs might take him days because he'd get sidetracked going

via Deniliquin, Booligal, Echuca or Mildura to see people he knew. It might be morning tea at Berriwillock, or lunch at Mildura but rarely a straight run and he'd often deliver items to people.

When he'd leave White Cliffs to return home, he always waited to get a tail wind at the back of the ute to blow him along home.

On the night he died in 1993, Allenby's trusty ute was loaded ready to leave Bendigo for White Cliffs in the early hours of the morning, but he and his beloved ute had travelled their final road together.

The night he died, the Datsun ute did too.

It had been a good and trusted friend but is now confined and resting in the backyard. Blue hopes it will be restored and working again one day. He throws nothing out and the ute will certainly never be sold. There are too many great memories tied up in the little old Datsun 1500 for one family to even think of parting with it.

It is one of the family.

Blondie & 'Murph'

I FIRST MET LINDA 'BLONDIE' MARSHALL at a ute show in southern Queensland in 1998. She is an avid ute lover - she gave herself an eighteenth birthday present called 'Murph' the ute.

'I almost purchased another HQ before I found my baby. Luckily, looking back now, it was sold before I could buy it and a mate rang me and said, "I think I have one, you'd better come and take a look". So I did.

'It was a fairly stock looking ute at the time. A white HQ, nothing real special, but it had a Statesman grille, a chrome three-inch rollbar and a set of side skirts. I was in love straight away. **I bought the ute that week and after affectionately naming it "Murphy's Law", we formed a long-term friendship. I look after him and he looks after me.'**

In the early days it was a six-cylinder. It had a 202 motor with a 186 head, a 350 Holley, five-speed gearbox and a Salisbury 3.08 diff, but to Blondie it was still a six. For two years Murph looked after her when she was an impoverished university student. Very little went wrong with the ute and for a ute that was then 25 years old, it was doing just fine.

'Murphy and I did some tricks in those first few years. We were always running low on time and lower on fuel. But we went everywhere. We even did the twelve-and-a-half hour trip down to the Hay B&S Ball. My "Mr Reliable" just kept on going.'

Then Blondie did the unthinkable by parking the ute in the shed for a year while she went to the Northern Territory. A mate started up the ute every couple of weeks and when she returned home, Murph was as good as new.

'A new clutch cable, oil and a bit of TLC, and we were on the road again, just in time for the Burren B&S. **Finally, it was time for Murph to move up in the world and the same mate who had found the ute in the first place gave me a 253 V8 motor for my twenty-first birthday!** He supervised me while I was rebuilding and we did the big change over. The love of my life was now a V8.'

Now a nice five-speed Supra gearbox makes Murph a dream on the highway,

while she likes the power you get in second and third gear around town. Other things are important to Blondie and her ute. **The first sticker on the ute was from her best mate and fellow B&S traveller; a simple sticker which reads, 'Protected by Smith & Wesson' - short and sweet.** She says the ute is everything she needs. It is a workhorse and a show pony all rolled into one. Now all it needed was a paint job and the four-year project would be finished.

'I have always said that he is the best man in my life (but not the only one) because he never cheats on me, never runs off with anyone else and is always there when you need him. He's my home when I'm not home. Everything I need fits in that ute. If it doesn't fit, I don't need it.'

Well, Murph has just received a new paint job and is now a 1999 Ford blue - a special colour mixed with metallic and pearl. 'I couldn't find a Holden blue I liked. The sunlight brings out the best in the colour.'

Since she bought it for about $3000, the ute has now been rebuilt for about $8500 - not bad really. Blondie did much of the work herself and she has learnt a lot about her ute in the process.

'I was interested to learn, but it was more a case of necessity really. I was at uni and was poor. I didn't know how to tell the difference between an HQ and a WB. Then I met an old bloke who owned a car yard, and he took an interest. He said, "Any ute you look to buy, bring it to me first and we'll put it up on the hoist and check it out". So we did that; he didn't want me to get ripped off. He sort of saw me as a daughter and he's always been a great help and has taught me along the way. I think he's very proud really. My uncle also taught me a lot.'

Blondie does have a very good knowledge of vehicles and is not afraid to get her hands dirty. She is very independent like her mother. She came from a home where **'There's nothing you can't do if you set your mind to it'**. She learnt that you either sink or swim, and if you swim you'll get there.

'Mum has always defended me and been very supportive. My sister, Bronwyn, and her husband have four girls aged 12, 10, 8 and 6. They all love Murphy the ute. **The second eldest niece says, "When I grow up, I want a ute like Auntie Linda's". Of course, I encourage them to save their money for one!'**

Blondie had plans for when the ute was newly painted. She planned to head off back to the Northern Territory again, but saw a job in the paper that interested her. She started the new job in Goondiwindi managing a pet store and saddlery business. **She loves animals and has two cats and a ute dog called 'Sam' – a 12-month-old female cattle dog that loves the ute and goes everywhere in it. Sam was most upset when the ute was missing while getting the new paint job.**

Blondie is going to make the best of the job and learn all she can. Any job can teach you things if you are interested, and when she eventually goes to the Northern Territory again, she will have that extra knowledge to take with her.

She has finished her university degree with a Bachelor of Applied Science, majoring in Home Economics. She plans to also do a Diploma of Education and will one day teach. Plenty of time for that later, though.

Her mother has worked on stations as a cook and naturally, Blondie learnt a lot while helping her mum out. So much so, that she too has worked as a cook.

'I first went to the Northern Territory as a governess, but when I was there, I ended up as second-round camp cook on 'Auvergne' station which is between Katherine (NT) and Kununurra (WA) and owned by Kerry Packer. I cooked for between 10 and 15 ringers and chopper pilots. It was great; I loved it.

'It was a bittersweet thing getting the new job in the pet store as now I won't get to go in Murph back to the Territory in the foreseeable future. Still, the people I work for now are great and if I want to do extra training, they'll help.'

I have no doubt that Linda Marshall – alias Blondie – along with Sam the dog and Murphy the ute, will make their mark wherever they go. An independent young lady with an education and an ability to 'have a go' will succeed. Besides, she has the world ahead of her. She has already achieved much in her 22 years.

She'd have to be a great bush Aussie - she drives a ute!

Go for it, Blondie!

INSURED BY SMITH & WESSON

'Bloody bewdie!' Deni ute muster

cable bloke

'If he's still there when I come back, I'll interview him,' I thought.

I WENT INTO THE FARM AND DID ANOTHER interview and about an hour or so later as I was leaving, saw the ute parked in the same spot next to a paddock fence-line, off the main road.

He might live on the New South Wales/Victorian border, but Dennis Compton could be almost anywhere working on the road. I found him on the job and headed for Port Campbell, in Victoria's southwest.

His business card says, 'Servicing the Murray & Goulburn Valleys and the Southern Riverina'. He has, however, worked as far north as Townsville and Cairns, locating underground cables. Another job was between Yass and Albury.

Much of the underground work involves optic fibre. Dennis goes with the engineer to locate underground services such as power, water and sewerage lines and liaises with local councils prior to the bulldozers and heavy machinery beginning construction.

Dennis was with Telcom for 22 years but he is now a self-employed contractor to big companies. He also does private work – telephone and modem socket installation, communication jointing and the location of underground cable faults. Dennis also operates a 24-hour emergency service. As his card says, 'One call does it all'. He left Telecom with many training courses under his belt and has a wide range of accreditations to stand him in good stead in this competitive world.

He was busy working and I knew not to stay too long; you don't stop a good man when he's hard at it. I let him continue working while I took some photos. He stopped long enough for a shot next to the ute, but then it was back to work. We swapped business cards, 'I'll ring you,' my often-used comment as we shook hands.

I left him to finish off then headed down the highway. I had many miles to go and he had a good four-hour drive ahead of himself in the afternoon.

We caught up a couple of months later.

His 'home away from home', the 1997 Toyota Hilux twin cab, carries everything he needs. It is loaded with clothing and personal gear in the back seat and all the necessaries for the jobs in the rear tray and in the trailer. When he is away from home, there has to be a fully functional workshop with him, and Dennis has a neat and well-equipped set-up.

'I like it. It has light steering and is really quite comfortable on the open road. It is disappointing on the hills, though, it really pulls back - even more so with the trailer on. It is a standard ute that I bought from a Toyota dealership. It was previously owned by a dairy farmer.

'Leaving Telecom after 22 years, it took some time to settle into working for myself, but you never know if you don't have a go. I have a young bloke of 17 and I thought this might be a business he could move into if he found it hard to get a job.'

Dennis and wife, Leigh, have three children – Aidyn, 17, Jason, 15, and Chelsea, 11. Of course, we can't forget the family dog, Bill, the seven-year-old German shorthaired pointer.

As I was interviewing Dennis he was only a few days from heading off for the annual Fathers and Sons fishing trip up the Darling River. This trip only three utes and six blokes are going while in the past there have been up to eight or nine. This year is the tenth anniversary trip. The ute even has a full canvas cover with the boat frame on the outside so it can be loaded on also.

'The dual cab is the best ever invented. Not only for my work, but also I take the dog down to the river most nights for a run, or the kids swimming. You have the extra seats and still have a ute.'

Craig's Cruiser

IT'S BEEN JUST ABOUT EVERYWHERE - and looks it - but to Craig Rogers it is a vehicle full of memories. A faded map of Australia painted on the bonnet shows a glimpse of some of the places the two have been.

Around the coastline of Australia, through the centre of the Outback, across the infamous Gunbarrel Highway and right up to the pointy bit at the top – Cape York Peninsula. And countless thousands of other miles all over this place we call home.

Craig Rogers was born too late. He belongs in a cowboy movie. Or better still, the real thing in the American West. His kitchen walls are covered in photos of John Wayne. The lounge walls have framed posters of various western movies and other memorabilia. With his partner, Sue, we sat in the kitchen and talked of movies. I too, grew up loving old western movies.

I loved Randolph Scott, Gary Cooper, John Wayne, Errol Flynn, Audie Murphy, Alan Ladd, Robert Mitchum, and just about any other who slapped on a six-gun. The first book I ever wrote was a western dime novel. It remains unpublished!

And who remembers who played the part of Rowdy Yates in *Rawhide*? I named my dog after Rowdy Yates. I even met the grandson of an old Hollywood cowboy once! I also met the bloke who did the stunts for Robert Mitchum in the movie *Thunder Road*. Ah, fame. Memories.

Anyway, we finally got to talking about his ute.

The 1984 HJ47 diesel Toyota Landcruiser tray-back was found after he'd spoken to a caryard salesman. Craig was looking for a ute to go around Australia in.

'He rang me to say he had got one in; a plain ute off a farm. I bought it the next day for $15 000 when it had 123 000 kilometres on it. I added a bullbar, SAAS seats, Sunraysia wheels and tyres, CB, overhead consol, towbar, canopy and a long range fuel tank of 128 litres. Now, though, it's got a 240-litre fuel tank.'

'I headed off first in 1990 to Adelaide, up the Birdsville Track, up to Mount Isa, to Longreach, the Strzelecki Track, Alice Springs, then right across the Gunbarrel Highway to Kalgoorlie. I was away 12 months on the first trip. I saw all the southwest of Western Australia, then right up to Broome, the Kimberleys, across the Top End, across to Brisbane, down the Darling River tracks, along the Murray through to Far East Gippsland then back home.

'I've crossed the Nullarbor about six times in the ute. I love the remote areas. It's been numerous times to the Northern Territory and to Western Australia. It did 50 000 kilometres in two and a half years. I always tried to get off the main roads too - deliberately off the bitumen. Now it has 336 000 kilometres on the clock.

'Crossing the Gunbarrel Highway it was in first gear for most of the 10 hours a day of travelling. If we got into second gear it was great. It took four or five days to drive about 700 kilometres to Carnegie Homestead.'

As a fitter and turner by trade, Craig never had any problems finding work in the mining industry as he travelled all over the country.

In 1994 the ute got a turbo and five-speed in the same week. 'Sensational,' says Craig. 'I did a clutch in it the other day. That's the first major surgery it has had in 11 years.'

And what does Sue think of the ute? 'Everyone looks at you in it; it's noisy, but I like it. It goes up and down hills. I prefer my car with auto and power steering, though.'

This is a ute that is used. Really used. It tows their twin horse-float. (They ride horses in the high country of New South Wales and Victoria.) It even pulls out trees on their bush block where they are building their new home.

Craig has countless memories of his travels. The best spots in Australia? 'The Kimberleys. Mitchell Plateau – amazing country.'

The hardest country? 'Cape York, I got stuck on Gunshot Crossing; roughest track I've ever been on – took 10 years off my life.'

Craig has had many adventures and has many yarns to tell. One is still strong in his mind.

'I was on Victoria River down near Top Springs. I was on my own when I blew a front RHD tyre, and then later the spare as well. The vehicle ran off the road and into a spoon drain and ploughed on through a few saplings. So I got the seat out of the ute and began to set up camp.

'Later a cook from a nearby station came past on his motorbike. He was totally pissed. He had a day off and was on his way to another camp to have a few drinks with his mates. He gave me a couple of

There are just too many stories about Craig's ute to relate here. There's the one about rolling it on its side going uphill, for instance. He was left dangling in his seat-belt. But that's another story for another time.

That's what I always find about people with utes – they always have a good story to tell.

Sue drives their Landcruiser Sahara wagon. She works as a clerk and Craig is now a truck and dog man, carrying sand from the quarries as a subcontractor for Boral.

Sue says of his ute, 'He treats it like a big truck and goes anywhere. He never washes it; he hits things and goes over anything and it still goes. You can do anything with it – and you do!'

And, of course, we couldn't forget to mention the two ute pooches 'Tessie', the seven-year-old Jack Russell fox terrier cross, and 'Miska' the 12-year-old Cavalier King Charles spaniel. They love the ute.

And finally Craig sums it up in one line: 'Good old ute, that.'

tinnies of hot beer and took off. He came back again on his way to work, still absolutely and totally pissed.

'About a day later a semi-trailer pulled up. The bloke said he wouldn't be back this way for three days, but if I liked, he would take the two rims and tubes and see what he could do. I gave him all the money I had on me – $300 as well as the two tubes and rims and watched him head off down the dusty road. I just didn't know if I'd see him or my money again. Anyway, in three days, sure enough, here he comes down the road. He gave me the wheels, all ready to put on, and then he says, "Here's your change - and here's your receipt!" I couldn't believe it. He wouldn't take anything for helping me out either.'

How's that for outback honesty?

Designer Dave

I CALL HIM A 'POMMIE BASTARD', BUT HE reckons that he's been in Australia for all but 15 of his 62 years. His family emigrated from South Devon, England, in 1955, so I guess I can't really call him a 'Pommie' now. It's about time you lost your accent, you old bush bastard!

He lives in the hills along a dead-end dirt track, but like many people today, he now works from home. Dave and his wife, Maureen, chose to leave the city in 1988 to build their own retreat in the bush. No mortgage, and Dave wanted to build the home himself. He is a building designer.

'I wanted to leave the city behind because of the lack of room, the narrow-mindedness of neighbours and the lack of opportunity to be an individual. We built and moved into the "original humpy" which has two bedrooms, living room, kitchenette, laundry, bathroom, woodshed and dunny,' says Dave. 'We hope to move into the new home by the end of the year.'

Dave has built a great home of bush stone, brick and slate. It is a credit not only to his skill but also to his perseverance. It is a home that will be filled with memories. The whole family have helped with the backbreaking task of man-handling huge slabs of slate and stone.

Dave did the architectural drawings for my new brick and stone, two-story office and garage and will do the new stone home attachment next. His own office is at the end of a walk up a winding dirt track through saplings, scrub and eucalypts. He built his design studio office and divided it to include space for Maureen's laboratory. Maureen is a vibrational herbalist working with plants to help 'alleviate pain and suffering', as Dave describes it.

'My grandmother got me interested in plants when I was just a little girl. She was a natural teacher and had multiple degrees in a time when women simply didn't. She was very inquisitive and

Dave has been designing for 46 years and now works mainly on residential and commercial projects. Over the years he has worked in most forms of the building industry including structural, shop, and factory design.

When I first met him some years ago, he had a ute which immediately caught my eye. A Ford XW with a ZC Fairlane front half.

'I bought it off a feral called "Herman" who had bought it off another mate. I offered him $800 for it and he jumped at it. I've built it up a bit and it's been here ever since. It's only been out the gate once since and that was for a load of slate. It hasn't been used much but I like it. I've had it for three years.'

The two-and-a-half ton Dodge truck did the heavy work around the place and when most of that was done, Dave decided he wanted to sell it and use the money to fully rebuild the XW ute.

Then another ute came into Dave's life – another Ford – this time an XB GS, with a 308 and running on gas. The bloke who wanted the truck also wanted to get rid of his ute, so they did a swap.

passed her interest onto me,' says Maureen. 'I've been working as a herbalist now for 26 years. It is all about balance. I make infusions, tinctures, essential oils, healing balms, unctions, sprays and creams.'

The scents and aromas of the oils and herbs around Maureen's laboratory are incredible. People come from all over the country and even overseas to consult her, requesting preparations to suit their needs. She is a well-known author on herbal arts and also lectures to assorted groups ranging from continuing education classes, to botanical groups, and even presents talks for inmates at the local prison.

As we sat yakking in the kitchenette, Maureen toasted hot-cross buns to go with the tea and biscuits. Then I heard the story of how the second ute came into the family.

'Mick-the-tattooed-feral wanted to go into work salvaging material from building sites but his ute was too small. I'd finished with the truck and so it was a good swap for both of us.'

So, for a man who, until three years ago, never owned a ute, Dave now owns two. 'Now I am a confirmed ute driver and prefer driving the ute to my Benz.' (Dave has a 500 SEL Mercedes Benz sedan and Maureen has a VW Kombi van.)

'You just gotta have a ute. How else are you going to take the bins to the tip if you haven't got a ute?'

With that profound bit of truth it was time to give 'Dog', the female eight-year-old cocker spaniel poodle cross (Dave calls her a cocker-spoodle!) one last scratch behind the ear and head down the dusty track.

Another ute yarn was complete. Dave and Maureen Timson's gate-sign, 'Woof-wood', was lost in the dust in my rear-view mirror.

The Dodge

IT'S NOT OFTEN I GET TO DRIVE UP A remote driveway in the hills and have a line of vehicles to welcome me. But when I heard about Stuart and Jane, that's what I was told to expect. They live on three acres in a bush setting in the hills surrounded by old goldfields.

'China', the dog, barked a welcome as I drove up the hill past the line of old vehicles and towards a restored cottage surrounded by all sorts of interesting sheds, a lovely garden and a garage and workshop.

Arriving here some 14 years ago when the house was in such bad repair, Stuart could only use the kitchen and nothing of the rest of the place. Since then and after a lot of work they have made a lovely home with warmth and charm.

When Stuart was making a stone verandah around the bush retreat called home, he was carting large flat bush stones in a 5 x 4 trailer, towed by an Austin A40 car. It didn't take him long to realise that it wasn't strong enough to tow such huge loads.

While reading through the *Trading Post* newspaper, he saw an advertisement that attracted his interest. The ad was for a 1956 Dodge 108A, and he knew he had to go and see it.

'I caught a train to a town a few hours away and the owner picked me up at the railway station in it. It started to rain just as I got there. It was either buy it or catch the train home.

'I wasn't overly impressed with it at first, but it was going, strong and cheap. It was just over $3000. Anyway, we went for a drive, and after some negotiating and thinking about it, I made up my mind. I bought it and drove it home.'

It is still pretty much as he bought it, although he replaced a broken crankshaft. Even with the broken one it still drove but with a 'clunk, clunk' sound. He found a crankshaft in a paddock and the old bloke who owned it gave it to Stuart.

He collected a few other extra bits for it too, and a friend gave him some extra aerials. At one stage he bought a box of stuff at a clearing sale, and continues to buy bits whenever they pop up.

'Old blokes often come up to me in the street when they see the Dodge and say, "I've got one of these in my paddock", and offer me stuff.'

Lining the driveway of Stuart's place is a 1949 Austin, a 1950 Fargo and a 1956 Dodge. Also in the collection is a 1957 Morris sedan, an 1965 Mercedes, an Austin A40 sedan and an Austin A40 ute.

He loves the ute. 'I like being up high. I like its strength – it'd pull over a house.

It's got a three speed on the column. It's perfect for carting stuff and friends have often asked for its help in moving their households. It's remarkably good for its age; I look after it and average about 80 kph.

'I can go pretty well anywhere in it on any bush track. It's pretty good on the road too; it used to wander a bit, but then an old bloke told me how to fix the steering box with grease rather than oil.'

After 14 years renovating the 1856 home in the hills, the ute has really played its part. It has carted absolutely heaps of material including nine-foot lengths of roofing iron for the work studio, loads of gravel, cement and material from clearing sales.

A favourite pastime is the lovely garden, which features many attractive stone walls. The ute has played its part in creating the garden too, carrying countless loads of topsoil and stone.

They would be lost without the ute.

Their ute pooch, 'China' as in 'china-plate', has a true blue Aussie nickname. He is eight years old and just walked in one day when he was still very young. He's a bit of a mixture of Fox Terrier and Red Heeler.

'Actually, he's taken a bit of a dislike to the ute since he fell off the seat and hit the dashboard. He's not too sure.'

He jumped in pretty quick, though, when we opened the door to take a photo of him. He's friendly, but he will growl if you get too close to the ute when he's in it. (Maybe he just didn't like the camera!)

They are very definite about their interest in the older stuff. He says he wouldn't buy a vehicle made after the '60s.

Stuart is an illustrator and an example of his work is the original drawing that appears on page 47. It shows how he hopes to see the ute when it is fully restored.

And let's give Jane the last word. What does she think of the ute?

'Oh, I love it, it's great.'

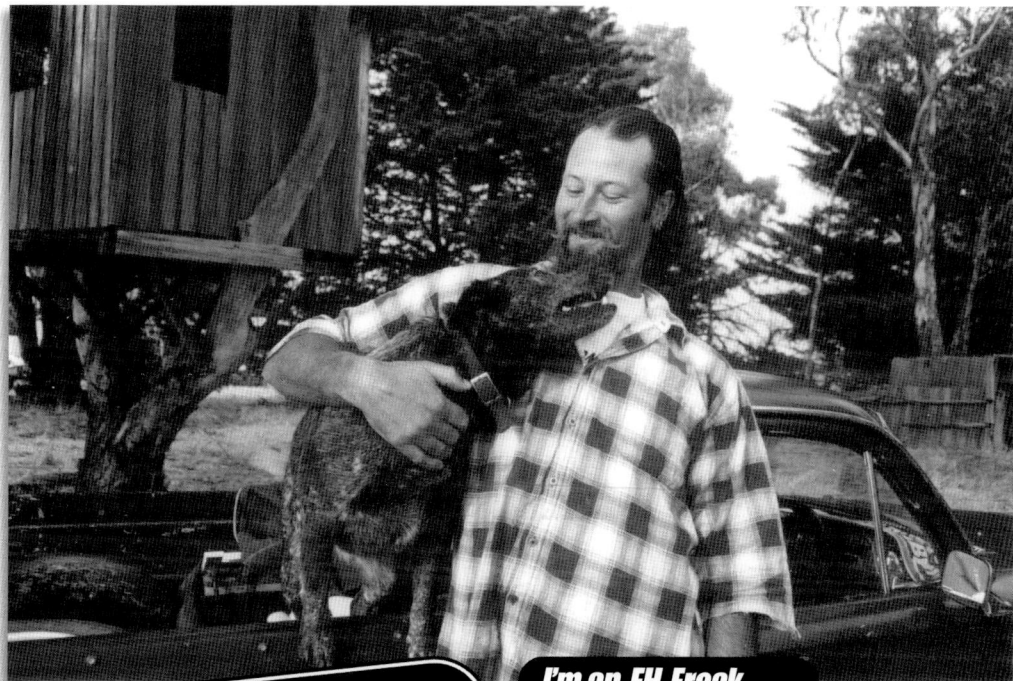

'EH' Freak

I'm an EH Freak

WELL, HE SAID IT, NOT ME AND I WOULDN'T call him a freak, just a lover of the great Aussie EH Holdens. He has six: a sedan with a 350 Chev in it, three utes, a panel van and a station-wagon!

Steven Jefferies really loves his EH Holdens, as well as the three or four motorbikes kept in one of the numerous garages on the family farm.

'I'm a qualified mechanic, but I now work as a service station attendant because my bad back forced me from my trade. I have a lot of bone and joint problems in the back and just can't do what I used to do. I'd love to get back into it again.'

Steven loves restoring but can only do a bit at a time. He is adamant that one day his vehicles will all be restored. He bought his first vehicle, a Holden EH panel van, when he was 17, not long before he got his licence.

'The EH was the first car I ever fell in love with. I actually got my first EH when I was 14. A man I was doing "work experience" for gave it to me. Because I was always down the back looking at it, he said I could have it as payment for the work I was doing for him. So I gladly took it.'

Steven, 30, is divorced with three much loved daughters, Sarah, 9, Sandy, 8 and Jayne, 7. His daily work vehicle is the deep red EH ute. A kid had bought it and was going to fix it up but he moved to the city, and so Steven bought it.

'I've spent most of the money so far on the motor - nearly $4000. It's got a 202 motor, 90 000 over Duralite pistons, balanced 370 cam, large valves, on ported head. All the usual stuff hanging off it: extractors, electric dissie, webbers. It's in the midst now of an interior "do up" – three gauges, ground steering column to get rid of shift. It's got chromies, 13 x 6 front and 13 x 7 back. It is a long-term project - want to see it straight as a die with a 253 V8 in it. I have that already sitting in the shed waiting for her.'

I asked him about his father's ute. [See One-Tonner 'JJ' on page 101] With a laugh, he says, 'It'd be great if he looked after it. I've built the motor and gearbox a couple of times. It gets washed about once a year!'

As you walk around the various sheds on the farm, you know this is a man who really loves EHs. Every shed has cars, utes, panel vans or motorbikes in it and underneath some trees there are other Holdens. The HX ute is now the 'paddock ute'. They use it for repairs to the fences and it's always loaded up with gear. There's also an EK and a few other bits.

HOLDEN HALF TON UTILITY

RIGHT OUT AHEAD IN GOOD LOOKS   IN NEW PRACTICAL FEATURES

The new Holden Utility! Latest model of the only utility specifically designed for Australia. No utility has ever been better to look at; better to drive; more thoroughly practical; more dependable; or more durably built. And because these qualities are combined with low list price, outstanding operating economy and the promise of a bigger return on your investment at trade-in time, the new Holden Utility is right out ahead in the value it gives you for your money.

In appearance, the new Holden Utility is completely modern, completely functional. It is more than four inches lower, yet it has the same ample ground clearance and there's full head room in the cabin for three 6-footers. Thanks to Holden's new, low-slung profile and longer rear springs, its riding, road-holding and handling are better than anything you've experienced before in a commercial vehicle. And Holden brings you many other new features for more

efficient operation. Improved manufacturing methods make the famous Holden six cylinder engine even smoother, even more responsive. The brakes are completely new, easier-acting and more powerful. The new electric windshield wipers have a parallel action to eliminate the centre blind-spot. And now Hydra-Matic automatic transmission is available at moderate extra cost as a factory-fitted option.

You'd have about as much chance of winning Tattslotto as you would getting him to sell anything to do with his Holdens.

In the house there are models of cars and utes and there are framed prints of EHs on the lounge room wall. On the kitchen cupboard his father has a set of six Peter Brock plates with images of Brockie and his various cars. This is one 'true blue' Holden family.

I had to ask: had the EH ever let him down? He was not real impressed. 'Mmmm,' he replied with downcast eyes. 'Once it had to be towed - worst part was it was towed by a bloody Ford. I still cop heaps of flack about it from my mates.'

As an owner of two EH Holdens myself, I'd have to agree. The EH is one of the best.

'I also love EHs because they are strong, easy to get parts for and bloody easy to work on.'

His final word on the subject? 'I just like the style.'

Ex-council Delmenico Dodge

'There are a lot of good memories and sentimental value in that ute.'

NEIL DELMENICO HAS A REAL SOFT SPOT for the 1968 Dodge ute that his father bought in 1970. The ute (built in May 1968) had been bought new by the Castlemaine City Council and was used by a Mr Dingwall in his job as sewerage and plumbing inspector.

'The Council traded it in after about 20 000 miles and Dad bought it from a local yard.' Neil's father, Jo, would have known its history because, at the time, he was also working for the Council.

Jo Delmenico was born in 1909 and was a gold miner at Wattle Gully mine. His first vehicle was an Oakland Tourer, which was cut down to make a ute. Prior to that he always had a horse and cart. Some years later he was working for a brickworks when the business was sold to a new owner who had a slate, sand and soil yard in Preston, Melbourne. The new owner

also took on the workforce, including Jo, who was then employed to extract slate from a local quarry.

Jo later became a self-employed quarryman. He eventually sold the truck he had been using to carry slate but when he joined the Council, he found that he still needed a vehicle to carry a bit of slate. So that was how he ended up buying the Dodge.

It was the good condition of the ute that attracted me to it in the first place. I spotted it, did a U-turn and followed Neil to the local garage where he was headed. We had a yarn and I caught up with him again a week later at his home, where we shared a 'cuppa' and biscuits with his wife, Melva.

When I asked her what she thought of the ute, she just laughed. 'It's good to ride in but I don't like driving it, and these gears and such - I like automatic.' I sense though, that she also has fond memories of earlier days.

'It will never be sold while we are alive,' she says and Neil is definite about that!

With two daughters and a son, hopefully one will keep it for its family history value. Their grandson, Nicholas Woodman, three years of age, should own it, I think.

'He is absolutely obsessed with it, and uses any excuse to get outside to see it. He says he wants a swing, so you take him into the yard, but he always asks to go in

the ute. He puts the seat belt on and steers it,' laughs Neil.

Now, *he* definitely sounds like a future uteman.

Neil Delmenico joined the police force in 1950. He has been stationed in many places and was Officer-in-Charge (OIC) at Maryborough, Second-in-Charge (2IC) in Bendigo, and was OIC at Castlemaine when they got their first police car. He has also worked at Russell Street police headquarters. He retired as Senior Sergeant in 1985 after 35 years.

'My father drove the ute from about 1970 and I took over in 1980. Not bad for a ute that's now 30 odd years old,' says Neil. 'When I took it over, a nephew had been using it for about 12 months. He was going pig shooting in it up near Moulamein. I thought it'd be better if I had it and ended up keeping it. I took Dad fishing in it a lot of the time - weekends to Lake Victoria, Rufus River, Barham, Moama.'

'Every weekend,' chips in Melva. 'They were real bushies, camped out on the river bank.'

The Dodge has always been a real work ute.

'When I retired, it became the "general hack". I was a rabbiter, fisherman, fruit picker - great hobbies and I made a few bob. The ute never let me down. It

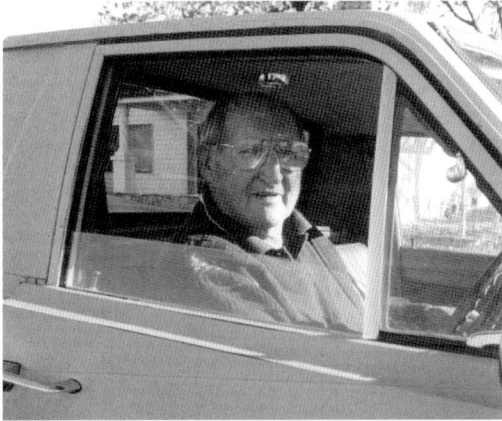

has no history of problems at all. I've always kept it in good order; it's serviced regularly.' (Neil has kept a diary of petrol and servicing.)

The day I first met him was outside the garage where it has been serviced all these years. That day it also turned over 90 000 miles on the speedo. It has had part of the seat re-upholstered. It had no heater or radio in it, but Neil has since put in a radio.

'It's just a good multi-purpose vehicle. I wouldn't like to dispose of it; it's so handy. You don't need to have a trailer to go out to the tip. A mate said to me once,

"You need a little Jack Russell for the ute, it'd look tremendous." Well, a neighbour's dog was sort of adopted by us and he loved to go out in the ute. He died of old age.'

And so it was time to leave the tea and biscuits and another happy ute-owning

home, with the smell of homemade, green tomato pickle firmly entrenched in my nostrils. Another ute and Aussie couple had shared their time and memories.

I left knowing that another great ute was in safe hands.

Exquisite! – Dodge & a Holden

I FIND UTES IN ALL SORTS OF PLACES ALL over Australia. When I found Ray Stevens on the side of the road with his ute one weekend selling hazelnuts and chestnuts, I thought it would be a nice story just to show yet another use for a ute. Little did I realise it would introduce me to a man who loves 'old stuff' like me and it would also add another ute to my own collection.

Ray was busy selling his produce and as I waited to talk, another two utes came around the bend, immediately did U-turns and pulled up.

The four young blokes wanted to check out my ute, 'The Mongrel'. As we talked, another ute pulled up. It was driven by a man who was on his way home - he wanted to see the ute and find out what all the fuss was about.

No sooner had he gone than a car pulled up; it was a bloke who often visited my website and had emailed me about his own ute. He wanted to say, 'G'day'. As we talked, a Nissan Patrol pulled up; it was a

bloke I had recently interviewed who wanted to know if I had time to go and see another ute.

That is what my life is often like nowadays - one ute leads to another and another. People know I'm a sucker for another ute to look at.

Ray was still selling his nuts and I think was rather amazed at the number of people who stopped by. Finally, I managed to organise a time to catch him at home when we were both not so busy.

A few days later I drove to see Ray. He was in his garage and the 1978 Holden HX one-tonner was in the driveway. Ray bought it brand new. He offered an old 1966 Cortina that was absolutely buggered as a trade-in. It practically had no brakes but the caryard salesman said, 'I'll have to take it for a test drive'. Ray laughed at the thought, but when he returned he was offered $600 as the trade-in price. Ray couldn't believe it.

'Two hundred and sixty thousand kilometres later it is still a bloody good ute,' says Ray.

It is the only ute Ray has ever owned. It was canary yellow, much to his wife, Norma's, disgust. As time wore on so the did the colour and Ray recently repainted it – canary yellow.

'It was shocking,' she says, 'faded paint and it even had the wrong phone number painted on it – one of our sons had his phone number painted on it for a while.'

Norma has driven the ute only once but she says she couldn't reach the pedals. Most blokes would like that; it's one

planted 300 hazel and chestnuts trees and now the property provides an interest and a place to store his gear. Ray is an avid collector of old machinery dating back to the early 1900s. He restores these machines to original condition and now has about 15 beautiful old engines. He is also a member of the local vintage machinery club.

We went out to the property on the edge of town because of something Ray casually mentioned during the interview. We were sitting at the kitchen table having a cuppa and biscuits. My ears pricked up when he mentioned another old vehicle. I was excited by what I was hearing. 'Do you still have it?' I asked incredulously. 'Yeah, it's out at the farm in the shed.'

'Well, fair suck of the sauce bottle and shiver me timbers,' I thought.

Some short while later he was unlocking the gate and the doors to the huge shed. And there it was. I fell in love straight away.

Sometimes you love to see a beautifully restored ute, brought back to its former glory, and I've seen hundreds of them. But this one is what I love to see also – one that is in its original condition, never touched other than to drive. Paint peeling,

way to keep the wife out of what most blokes think of as their pride and joy or their beloved toy.

'It is a great ute for him to cart all his junk in, though. "Steptoe", I call him,' she laughs.

Ray has different thoughts about the ute. 'It's very useful; the average person only buys a ute for what they can use it for. I bought this ute because, at the time, I had a business and I needed a ute to carry truck tyres and all sorts of other stuff. We used it to go fishing and duck shooting.'

In 1980 he bought a nine-acre property with several old sheds and the like. 'A beautiful little place that I could live on happily – in one of the great old sheds.' He

dust and a heap of junk thrown on the back of it; two front wheels missing and resting on two blocks of wood.

A 1924 Dodge ute.

Now, before all you wheelers and dealers start to drool, too late! So don't annoy Ray for it or anything else. One day it will be on permanent show in the Beaut Utes Museum. You have about as much hope of buying it from me as winning Tattslotto, the Melbourne Cup and the Sydney to Hobart yacht race all in the one day!

So what is the history behind the original old Dodge?

'It was bought new by an old farmer, Jim Egan. I got it off him about five years before he died at 89. I've had it for about 17 years now. I used to collect milk from his farm. He would drive the ute out to the gate and I'd collect the cans. One day I said, "Why don't I pick the milk up straight from your dairy; that'll save you worrying about it?" He was very pleased and so I did from then on.

'Jim knew I liked the old ute - I offered to buy it but he wouldn't sell. But old Jim was getting pretty old. One night the phone rang and he said, "Stevo, if you don't come and get it, you won't get it."

'I went out the next day and he actually gave it to me. For nothing.'

Ray is known as 'Stevo', 'Bill' and 'Chief', but whatever name he's associated with, one thing is for sure: everyone knows Ray's interest in the preservation of anything old. Like me, he collects just about anything so long as it is from a bygone era. That's probably one reason we hit it off so well.

He even got the local preservation society to donate some of their proceeds to the old folks' home to buy a wheelchair. As he says, without those old people, they would not even have a preservation society.

Now 71 years young, Ray left school early and went tomato picking. He later travelled all over the country installing underground cables for three years. Then he had a stint at surveying and then for two years he was a milk cooler in a large dairy. He later became a driver collecting milk from farms over a wide area.

Finally, he bought his own truck and for 20 years he carted Caltex industrial oils to hospitals and factories. In 1975, when natural gas made oils less popular, he bought the first of a number of cranes, ranging from nine to 20 tonnes. For about 11 years he had a very successful business doing all sorts of construction work, even working on the building of a huge reservoir to supply water. He then sold the business and bought a cherry picker, continuing to work in the construction game and cutting trees for about seven years. A man never afraid of hard work and long hours, Ray also worked as a part-time bus driver. He officially retired in 1995.

Ray and Norma will celebrate 50 years of marriage shortly. They have two sons, Tony and Mark, as well as a granddaughter and two grandsons.

Ray might have slowed down a bit but I don't think he'll ever really retire. He is always out at his farm tending to the 300 trees or working on another engine. The beautiful garden he leaves to his Norma.

'I could have sold my ute many times - everyone wanted to buy it – but I didn't. I was going to once but changed my mind and I'm glad I still have it. Mechanically, it's perfect. I'd like to put an automatic in it now, though.'

Ray Stevens couldn't live without a ute.

'A good general vehicle, the ute. They are good for carting stuff for people. My sons have used it and they thought it was marvellous.'

This interest in utes will live on in the family – his grandson also has a Holden one-tonner.

HIS UTE HAS EIGHT CIGARETTE LIGHTERS
- and he doesn't even smoke!

Thorold Lee might live in the western suburbs of the city but his heart is in the bush, and he loves nothing better than heading for far northwestern New South Wales country, where he goes wild pig and goat shooting with his mates.

When he goes bush, there's very little terrain that 'Foz' can't cross. His ute is specially built – a one-off that has every conceivable gadget. Being prepared when he goes bush is Foz's best motto. Reliability is everything. Access all areas.

The ute is a 1968 XT Ford Falcon sitting on top of a 1978 FJ55 long wheelbase Toyota Landcruiser chassis, with the wheelbase extended an extra six-and-a-half inches. The suspension is also repositioned to suit.

'I knew nothing about vehicles what-so-ever before I built my other showcar Torana, but everyone in my neighbourhood was into cars and so I decided to have a go, too. But if I had my way over again, I'd never have even started building the ute. Too much stress,' says Foz.

A storeman for the last 18 years with an arts and craft supplier (selling everything from glue to paint, stationery, books and such) 34-year-old Foz is single and is always kept busy at work and after hours.

At work, it's packing and taking phone orders, stock control, loading and unloading trucks and doing deliveries all over the

place. He also worked for a few years as a roadie for the underground rave-party scene.

After hours, he spends time working with vehicles and is a keen internet surfer. Weekends, he heads bush or to the nearest car event or ute show.

'It was about 1987 or '88. Everyone was into illegal and legal street drags, but I was the only one just dagging around, so I thought I'd learn. Ever since then, I've pulled heaps of motors apart and I just wanted to prove I could learn and I learned fast. I've been at it ever since. I also did rallycross driving with my mates and raced competition motocross.'

The first major job he undertook was a Holden LH Torana. The motor came via a mate in a metal recycling yard. It had been a Holden test engine that was supposed to have been destroyed. He got the block for nothing and built up a 400 hp 308 for $7500. 'I did the works: shaved Brocky heads, big cam, flat-top, forged pistons, every part new and balanced and blue-printed, roll-caged and detailed for the show circuit. I bought an SLR 5000 mock-up sedan for $2500. Now it has had about $25 000 spent on it.'

In 1996 an uncle sold Foz the standard 'stock as a rock' XT ute for $1500. It had a small rollbar on it for shooting.

Foz rang an engineer for information, then bought a landcruiser for $2500, took the body off leaving the bare chassis with wheels, steering, suspension, bullbar and gearbox/transfer case. There were only a couple of inches difference in length between the XT and the 'cruiser' chassis, so he trailered it to a mate's place.

Reno, the engineer who became Foz's mate, hadn't built a vehicle like the one Foz wanted before either, but they started work. After much learning, many heartaches and late nights, and just on $25 000 later, the ute was passed - fully engineered and on the road in August

1996, just six months after they started building it.

She's a high rider - from the ground to the under sills is 80 centimetres *[32 inches]*, and from the ground to top of the roof is two metres *[6.2 feet]*.

There's a list a mile long of things that have been done to the ute; far too many to name them all here. But for the technically minded, here are just a few items: the ute has a fully balanced, rebuilt-from-the-ground-up, 250 2V Ford engine with a Holley 350 carbie, high pressure oil pump, reversed sump, pick up

and mild cam. The motor is set back two feet from the grille, with part of the motor actually sitting inside the vehicle because of front tailshaft restrictions.

It has a special starter motor and dual fuel (a 90-litre gas tank, two petrol tanks – a 70-litre and also one with a 57-litre capacity). The ute only gets between 10 and 15 miles to the gallon.

There are two fuel pumps, two fans (one normal, one turbo-thermo), two batteries, dual horns, two ignition systems, two ignition coils, Alfa Romeo bucket seats,

phone, CB, UHF, radio cassette, CD, VDO clock and inclometer, engine management gauges, fire extinguisher, medical kit, extra portable plug-in heater/demister. And of course, there are numerous large bull-lights on the bullbar.

There was a canopy in the back, but Foz has now removed it and gone for a rollbar. Also in the back are a lock-up toolbox and a 48-inch jack. The snorkel is made from a 3-inch chrome exhaust pipe with a manual override for extra air intake. The wheels are 32-inch x 9-inch ROH with all-terrain tyres. There is a long list of 'special made' parts on this ute - brackets, clutch, braking system and more.

'Halfway through the project I nearly stopped. I was too stressed out. I had an ad written out for the FOR SALE column, but then I changed my mind, screwed the paper up and threw it away. I am now pretty satisfied with it - it was a long, hard haul. Now I just turn the key and go, but once I used to stress out whether it would go or not.'

Foz is a sensible driver who hasn't had a speeding fine since 1993. He refuses to drink and the ute will never be doing circle work. She's a bit top heavy; and

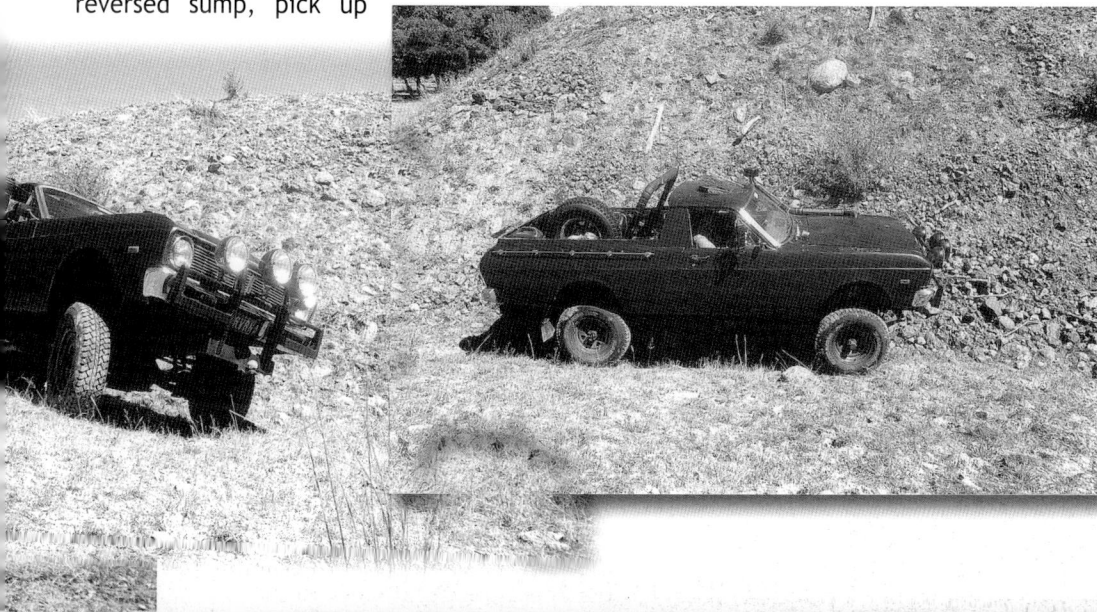

XTricky 4X4

built for rough bush travel. She gets plenty of that when Foz heads out shooting to places like the big stations near Deniliquin, Bourke, Cobar and all the way up to the Queensland border. He always looks for new bits to add, and the day I interviewed him, he had just installed a sunroof that he bought for $10 at a swap meet. A mate helped install it, which cost Foz a bottle of scotch and $20 worth of waterproof sealant.

'As soon as I get off the bitumen, I'm right at home; that is what it was really built for. It goes anywhere - places where normal four-wheel drives wouldn't even want to go.'

He is pretty understated when it comes to the vehicle but everything on it has a job and must be working. His ideas are put into practice. 'I am a storeman with no qualifications at all, but a lot of ideas which I set out to achieve.'

Pretty impressive, Foz. But why all the cigarette lighters, especially for a bloke who doesn't smoke?

'They run all sorts of spotlights and anything that needs power. One in the back runs a spotlight that has 30 feet of lead so you can walk away from the vehicle and still have light. Others are in the engine bay, in the cab and wherever needed.

And why the number plates NRVRNA?

'When Nirvana singer, Kurt Cobain, died in 1994, I bought the plates as a tribute to him. I used to be a radio announcer for seven years playing that type of music.

And his ute is to Foz what NIRVANA stands for - 'PURE BLISS'.

Gone... but not forgotten!

I PULLED OFF THE HUME HIGHWAY AND decided to go for a quiet cuppa and toasted sandwich before moving on a few hundred more kilometres.

Jugiong, New South Wales, is one of those towns that has been bypassed. I pulled into the front of a small roadhouse and went inside. I noticed a woman get up from her table and come over to the window near where I was now sitting.

'That's a really nice ute,' she said. She mentioned that she had once had a ute but it had been stolen. Hey, if anyone's got a story about a ute, I'm all ears.

We were all talking about utes, travel, houses and more, while I had my sandwiches and tea.

As Ian and Ellinor Robertson were about to leave, I asked if she would mind if I interviewed her about her ute. No worries. They have houses in Sydney and Melbourne and Jugiong is a good halfway stopover. They hope to eventually live here full-time.

Dennis, the 14-year-old cattle dog, and Delores, the 7-year-old black Labrador, greeted me and were happy to welcome a newcomer to their yard.

Ian, a successful businessman, is an importer of industrial food equipment – machinery to make hamburgers, continuous cookers, meat mincers and the like – for big companies such as Ingham Chickens, Steggles and Don Smallgoods. The Robertsons are serious world travellers. They lived in Hong Kong for two years, and have been to America, the Middle East, Israel, Asia, the Philippines, Egypt, Tokyo and over the North Pole. Every year they go to countries in eastern and western Europe.

Ellinor is a horticulturalist and she wanted a ute to transport things around. They have also been doing up houses together for years so the 1994 VR Holden ute suited their various purposes very well.

Originally a Canberra ute, they bought it from a caryard on the Pacific Highway in Sydney when it had 47 000 kilometres on it. It was used in the construction industry. It had the original sun visor on it and it was Ellinor's first ute ever. She loved it.

'I used it to carry everything from my books when studying, to plant materials for the nursery called 'Gardens Are Us' where I worked for four years. After two years I got my certificate and after three years completed an Advanced Certificate of Horticulture.'

Ellinor later had her own business doing garden maintenance, planting, pruning and more. 'The ute was a very important part of my business,' she says.

During house renovations the ute was also important for carrying bricks, building timbers, cement and other materials. It travelled to the tip often – 'Dennis', the dog, always on board too.

'Once at the tip,' recalls Ellinor 'a big council dumpster truck drove into me. I was furious, I just couldn't believe it.'

The ute was involved in a robbery with Ellinor at the wheel. Ian says, 'My wallet had been just stolen. I spotted the thieves in the street and took off after them.'

'Ellinor jumped in the ute to chase them,' says Ian. 'Wherever they went, she turned up in the ute and finally I caught up. I got a black eye and the crap beaten out of me. Ellinor mounted the footpath in the ute.'

Ellinor became very coy about this time and I don't think she wanted to go into the full details. I gather the ute did its work and the thieves finally took off, leaving Ian bruised. They found the empty wallet in a nearby front yard.

'The ute saved me,' says Ian.

Then came 4 April 2000. It was four in the morning. Ian had borrowed the ute and taken a couch from Sydney to Melbourne. He had it parked in the street in front of their new place in Moonee Ponds. He awoke to a loud bang.

'Gees, that sounds like the ute,' thought Ian. 'Sure enough, there were two gentle-men with me sitting there open-mouthed watching as they drove it away,' said Ian.

He phoned the police who told him to come in and make a written report. On the following day Ian phoned Citylink and can-celled his e-tag (the electronic toll system used on Melbourne's new freeways) so the thieves couldn't use it. Too late, they had already used it extensively that day. Police said they couldn't do anything with the e-tag details, even though Citylink suppos-edly took photos of the vehicles each time it passed through a toll point. Ian had hoped that these photos may have identi-fied the thieves.

'I made several calls to police over the next few weeks,' says Ian. 'I contacted the district commander and car theft squad detectives. The ute was registered in New South Wales, so I rang the police there – no news.

'Looking back now, I remember seeing a bloke in an identical ute parked opposite our place in Melbourne. He was sitting there watching and talking on a mobile phone. I even wrote the rego down at the time, but when the ute was stolen, the half-witted detective didn't even bother to check it out.

'I even checked stolen car lists in New South Wales. Not even listed. No one seemed to care. It was insured so we got another vehicle, but it was not the same.'

Ellinor still seems pretty sad about it all. 'It even had beautiful new tyres on the back,' she laments. 'Ever since then I reckon I've eyeballed every white ute in Melbourne, trying to spot it. There will certainly be another ute in the family.'

'I used to love it if anyone revved at the stoplights; I would rev the ute too. I reverted back to being a hoon.'

Sounds like Ellinor is a closet rebel. Maybe that's why she also had a Eureka flag sticker in the centre of the tail-gate. I, of course, had to show them my ute with its southern cross flag that is part of my 'Uteman' logo.

Again it was time for me to hit the highway. We said our goodbyes, the dogs got their last pat from me and Ian had one last comment to make about their ute.

'Hello, wherever it is - our compli-ments!'

Gronow Utes

THERE ARE FOUR UTES IN THE BACKYARD at the Gronow property where the family share farms, milking a mixture of 250 friesian and jersey cows. I'd heard from a mate about one of these utes in particular. But I only had rough 'general district' directions on how to find the place, so we ended up on the side of the road trying to get directions from another farmer.

We had no name, no phone number, but knew roughly where a brother lived. We didn't know his name either, but we did know a bit about one of the utes. A bit of general deduction and thinking - and the farmer had worked out who it might be.

He gave directions and we headed off down a dirt road hoping to find the place.

Eventually, it was decided that we'd gone too far and we turned around to go back to the last farm we had passed. They had some utes to look at anyway, by the looks of it. As we drove closer we saw a ute in the carport - it was the farm we had been looking for in the first place.

Sometimes chasing utes can be a bit vague and sometimes it is just a matter of luck. There in the carport was the ute we were after - a 1947/8 Ford ute.

I pulled into the driveway behind the ute. A Blue Heeler dog, a young boy and his father were there waiting.

Jeff and Vicki Gronow have Lee, 18, Ryan, 14 and Luke, 5 to keep them busy, as well as the cows, and the breeding cocker spaniels and the three farm dogs. 'Blue'

was all ready for a pat and gave a few barks to say 'Howdy'. I went and introduced myself to 'Beau', the long-haired kelpie cross, who was still on the chain near the house. A good talk and a pat and we were mates, too.

We talked about the old Ford as Jeff showed it to us. He lifted a battery into place and fired it up. A deep, throaty V8 sound sprang to life. Music to the ears.

'In 1970 Dad was on holidays at the Albury caravan park and saw it. They had been using it to collect the rubbish bins around the park. Dad had had one before

and when he saw this one, he had to buy it. He planned to do it up, but he got it home and until last week it has been sitting in the shed and has never been used for the past 21 years. I got it out of the shed to bring back home when I knew you were interested in it. I cleaned the carbie out; it was full of junk. I replaced a small piece of fuel line that the rats must have chewed through - and away she went.'

A good original old ute; a heap of old parts thrown in the back - just a good plain but very nice and worthy ute of bygone days. I photographed the rest of

the utes until drizzling rain finally drove us inside for a cuppa and some cake and biscuits. I learnt more about the rest of the utes.

The Subaru Brumby:

'I swapped a Holden 173 motor and got her for it. For the last two years she has been getting the cows in from the paddocks. A neighbour calls her the "heated Honda". When you are out there in the paddocks on a cold frosty morning, who wants to ride a motorbike and freeze? The ute is heated and that'll do me,' says Jeff with a laugh.

It is a ute that has had hard times and seen a few gate posts up close, as the dents in the back testify. Even 14-year-old Ryan has left his mark on it.

The Holden HQ:

'We left the exhaust behind one day,' laughs Ryan. It's obvious that the family all have memories of ute adventures of one sort or another. One that they all laugh about now is when the HQ got bogged while Jeff was out cutting wood. Jeff shakes his head.

'I was dodging lignum as I was driving through the scrub. We were out cutting wood and I backed up as it was getting boggy near the swamp, and as I dropped the clutch and gave it heaps – "Oh, shit!" – down she went, further into the swampy ground. I didn't have the phone with me.'

Ryan was only about seven or eight years old then; he was learning to drive. I asked Ryan to let the clutch out slowly while I gave the ute a push from behind, but he dropped the clutch and 4000 revs later, we were down to the axle quick as a flash.'

It seems Dad was not in the best of moods on that occasion. They had to hand-winch it out of the bog; no tractor or 4WD to pull them out.

'We're of the pioneering spirit out here,' laughs Vicki.

Jeff shakes his head and continues. 'We've had the HQ for 10 or 11 years, bought it privately when it had 118 000 miles on it. Spent little on it, except when we bought it; a new paint job was needed then, as all the previous owner did was to get out a spray can of silver-frost coloured paint and spray anywhere it needed painting. It was multi-coloured and looked awful.' Jeff is casual but pretty keen on his HQ, I think.

'It was rugged but it had potential,' says wife, Vicki.

Jeff says, 'I got the angle grinder and cut the rust out. It's now got a 253 V8 in it, and she's a good ute. Nothing much goes wrong with utes and they are easy to work on anyway.'

The 1965 Toyota Crown:

'Saw an ad in the paper and went and bought it. Had it before the HQ. When I got it home, I decided there was too much to do to get it up to scratch. I'd previously had a 1966 Crown ute, but there was a difference and so I ended up taking the Holden 161 motor out of the Crown and putting it into this one. It is not a bad old bus, and Ryan uses it as a paddock ute.'

I commented on how it didn't have any dents in it and young Ryan replied, 'Not yet!' He also added, 'You have to pump the brakes a few times before they take up and work; even then it takes 100 metres to stop.'

Something tells me he'll have a good excuse to tell Mum and Dad when he brings it home with a dent in it.

I asked Jeff how old he was when he learnt to drive, as most kids in the bush get to learn early. Jeff says he would have been around 10 or thereabouts. He used to belt round the paddocks in an old 34 Chev of his father's, and later in a Morris Minor.

Jeff is a plumber by trade, but gave it away to do maintenance work at a piggery for seven years, and has now been on the 400 acres for 13 years, share farming their dairy cows.

And what do utes mean to good country people like the Gronows?

'Can't do without them.'

jasmyn

IF YOU WANT TO HAVE A YARN WITH Jasmyn Crimmins, you'd better be prepared for a long drive. The first time we arranged to meet, we missed each other by two days. I finally got to photograph her ute on the side of the road near a country town, where we did an interview under a huge tree.

She grew up between Victoria's Little Desert and Big Desert country, her family home now is near Nhill, her ute is registered in Western Australia and she works 'anywhere' in outback Queensland. Her home is her ute - she travels with all her possessions in the back.

When she left her family two-and-a-half years ago, she went to work in the Kimberleys of far northwest Western Australia. Now, 200 000 kilometres later, she knows the bush pretty well. She has travelled to the Kimberleys four times and three times to Queensland.

If you look at a map of Queensland, you soon get to see why this 21-year-old young lady has to be independent and self-reliant. Jazz works as a child carer on big outback stations. She is employed by Frontier Services (a division of the Uniting Church). Remote Family Care Service (RFCS) and Remote Area Family Services (RAFS) are two programs run in conjunction with each other. Her 'territory' is some of the remotest country of Queensland to the Northern Territory border.

Some of the stations she has worked include: Melinda Downs (north of Cloncurry), Floraville (south of Burketown), Rocklands (Camooweal), Montague Downs (Boulia), Durham Downs (Noccundra), Yambutta (Eromanga), Mowellan (Cunnamulla), Nocatunga (Noccundra), Norley (Thargomindah), Kenmore (Mitchell), Wetlands (Augathella), Kihee (Eromanga), Tandarra (Morella, between Longreach and Winton), Riverview (Claremont), Westward Ho

(Boulia), Armraynald (Burketown), and Bingara (between Eulo and Thargomindah). She has also worked on Brunette Downs in the Northern Territory and other big stations as well.

'I am responsible for looking after kids from zero to five years old and helping with the general well-being of the family. I bath kids, make them meals, fix their toys, feed babies, clean clothes, but usually end up as a sort of jack-of-all-trades. I do things like cooking and gardening and organising activities. I often push cattle in stockyard work and I also fix up fences around vegetable gardens when stock break them down. I have learnt a lot about fixing vehicles and water pumps, but normally I don't do general maintenance work. And I don't do toilets. That's worked out when I start!

'Sometimes I might help the father with the bookwork on the computer. The kids are the main priority, though. I organise nature walks and craft activities and I teach them "School of the Air". They listen to "Flying Doctor on-air" half an hour a day, and I motivate them to work through the school manuals that are sent to them. They usually work through five lessons.

I have anything from pre-schoolers (four-year-olds) to Grade 6 (12-year-olds).

'The Royal Flying Doctors are great. I got bad tonsillitis at the Boulia Camel Races, and the RFDS doctor came out and looked after me. On stations, we have an RFDS medical metal chest. I've used heaps from that. I have to get signed permission from parents before I can administer medicine to kids from the RFDS kit.'

Jazz is sent an itinerary of her next job, the names of the people and reason for employment. It might be that the mother has just come home from hospital, or there's a sick child. Her usual stay on a station is for a maximum of only three weeks before moving on. For a family to be eligible, there must be at least one child under the age of five on the property.

She is one of 14 full-time carers supervised by Jasmine Jones, co-ordinator for Frontier in Townsville, who left Lake Boga in Victoria to work in Queensland. Frontier Services is always looking for more carers.

'The worst aspect is trying to help a mother who isn't coping, but at the same time, the most rewarding part of my job is to give a mum a break – to help a family and the kids survive. Teaching a 10-year-old kid, who's never seen a skipping rope, how to skip. Many isolated kids don't have good skills. They don't cope well in towns or with other kids.

'I've worked in itinerant workers' camps where you sleep in a swag in the back of a truck with all the family right next to you, through to fencing camps where some kids don't ever go anywhere except to the fencing jobs. I've also put on playgroups in Aboriginal communities.'

Jasmyn is a lady with a big heart and a smile to match. 'You make the best of where you are. I sometimes work 16-hour days, no overtime and often in tough conditions. The one thing this job teaches you is how to get on with people. I now know how to keep my eyes and ears open, and my mouth shut at times, too.'

The family farm that Jasmyn left is 2500 acres of prime cropping land between Nhill and Lake Hindmarsh where stepfather Peter, her mum, Kaye (who is a nurse) and family grow wheat, canola, beans, peas, lentils and legumes. Her brother Mark, 22, is a steel fabricator and welder in Melbourne. She misses her little sisters Elsa, 6, and Amy, 2. Her mother misses Jasmyn, but both her mum and Peter are very supportive. Jasmyn's whole community misses her.

Jasmyn studied agribusiness at Marcus Oldham College (near Geelong) where she learnt accounting, economics, maths,

plant studies, animal husbandry, work-place relations and computing. She has also worked as a cook.

'I left college but I will complete the course later on. For now, I am getting that real knowledge and first-hand experience they were trying to teach from books. I have learnt so much out here.'

And how does Jasmyn travel all those miles in the remotest of areas? Three years ago she bought her Atlantic blue 1978 HZ Holden ute. It has a 253 V8, on gas, and a bullbar that she is in love with. Bench seat ('Gotta have a bench seat!'), GTS dashboard, but no air-conditioner.

'What's a window for?' she laughs. 'I have a spray bottle of water to do my face and then I stick me head out the window in the wind,' she laughs again. The other 'long haul' requirement is the CD player. 'I'm a big Slim (Dusty) fan. Once on a long trip, I was low on cash and, at the time, I only had a Smokey Dawson CD. I listened to it non-stop for two days. I love old Smokey and often think of that mad trip home halfway across Australia.

'Utes are the most versatile vehicles, nothing like a country person in a ute; they don't flash it. Hate city kids in utes;

all tricked up and they've never had their boots dirty.'

The ute is always full - toy box for the kids, a big box for shoes, toolbox, medical kit, swag. The tray is carpet-lined. Everything is in bags made from wool-packs; keeps out the dust and keeps stuff dry. She carries three cans of petrol and 40 litres of water. The ute takes 50 litres of petrol and 70 litres of gas.

Once, she was headed for Nocatunga when the ute boiled, so she threw some pepper in the leaking radiator. It worked until she got to where she was going. Jasmyn has learnt a lot of tricks for staying safe in the Outback.

'I've been bogged Outback, but I always ring ahead and tell them when I will arrive. I've only had two flat tyres on sharp, stony roads. I don't 'boot it' along, just go with the road conditions. I have hit two kangaroos. I've driven 1300 kilometres in a day, arrived to play with the kids, then to bed and then up at 6 am to get into it again. I am now onto a second motor. Sometimes, I might work two months straight with no days off.'

Jasmyn dreams of owning her own 4WD Landcruiser and she is also looking for

'that man out there waiting.' Travel in the Outback has broadened her knowledge.

'I find it hard to talk to people down south about my job, they don't have wide experience and people of the Outback are great. They are friendly, beautiful people.'

She celebrated her twenty-first birthday at the Birdsville Races, and has been to 30 B&S Balls. 'Before I die, I want to serve on a B&S Committee'. They could get no harder worker than Jasmyn. She has a positive attitude to life. Her advice to all you people of her age: 'Get out and have a go, eh? Try real hard, even if you are knocked back. Love what you are doing, put a smile on your face and don't think about the negatives.'

This lady practices what she preaches and is a credit to herself and her family. With a get-up-and-go attitude, she is one of those strong Outback women - quite capable of looking after herself and others.

Go for it, Jasmyn - you're a legend in the making!

Just TWO UTES
- & a perfect comeback

UTE LOVERS ACROSS AUSTRALIA HAVE A real passion for their own particular ute and many hundreds of letters, emails and entries to the Uteman website give me an idea of how wide-spread this love of the ute is. But two entries just have to be related here.

One bloke is a bit of a brag; he titled his story *Australia's Most Powerful Ute* – a big claim and we reckon he might be trying to have a bit of a lend of us. Wal, on the other hand, has that down-to-earth, dry sense of humour that has earned him a place in ute lovers' hearts with his classic reply and description of his beloved ute.

Thanks, fellas, for your contributions.

(Wal - you win, mate.)

Crazy's ute

My ute has to be the most powerful-est ute in Australia. It's got a GReddy [sic] boost cut controller to allow 16 psi and an Aquamist water injection system. Air-to-air intercooled twin turbos. Moroso cold air kit, throttle boy air foil, and a 160 degree Hypertech powerstat, 150Db, show-winning MTX stereo with display lights, polished 3-inch twin Mandrel bent exhaust. Every bolt in car replaced with stainless cap screws. Does the standing quarter in the mid 12s and can pull a lateral acceleration of no less than 1.3 gs! I might be bringing it (if insurance permits) and if I do she'll be purring the whole trip. Circlework ain't part of this ute's life...yet! It's attached to a fully stroked 5.7 litre LS1 motor...it puts out 345 kws at the rear wheels.

Wal's ute

My ute is quite possibly the most piss-poor, unpowerful ute in the country. It's got a clapped out, old 308 with noisy tappets and a turbo 350 that is probably on the way out. I've replaced most panels with a fair dousing of bog and steel wool and most bolts have fallen out and been replaced with tek screws (God bless their invention). The stereo doesn't really work, but it's got two speakers, one with the cone broken. The other one works if I hit the head unit hard enough. It's got a two-and-a-half inch press bent exhaust with one muffler that had the front pipe pulled out of it when I got it beached on a bank on the side of the road and reversed off it. It does a quarter mile, which is the length from our house to about halfway down our track, in about three or four minutes, depending on whether the sheep are in the paddock or not. When I pull up at the pub, it pulls about 7 or 8 gs, depending on how many people are looking and say, 'Gee'. I reckon our utes are heaps the same; we should meet each other some time. PS: It's for sale.

Max & the 'FB'

I FIRST MET MAX WHEN I SAW HIS UTE parked on the nature strip - he was building a picket fence. I stopped for a yarn and it came out in conversation that his wife and I were distant relatives. We'd never met and it was pure chance. See what happens when you talk to ute drivers?

Max Graham was born in the country.

As a kid at High School in 1952, he remembers the train going past loaded with the first of the Holdens on their way to Adelaide. There were rail truck loads of them, and it made an impression on Max. He has always loved them.

He left school when he was 14 and worked on the family farm before going to Victoria's Mallee region to work on the harvesting trucks. In 1959-60 he was working on a station as a tractor driver and quietly saving his money to buy a new ute. He drooled over the Mark II Zephrs. The local water bailiffs had them but they were £100 more than the Holden, so he thought he'd buy one of those instead.

Max was 20 years old and his new pride and joy was an FB with buckskin tan duco and red trim. It cost £1070. He couldn't

afford a radio. He saved up to later buy the mudflaps and sun visor. 'It was a pretty nice ute,' says Max. 'I always looked after it.'

Max only got one Saturday off per month and he had to travel to Kerang to get the ute from agents, Hall & Sons. He returned to his employer's station and put it in the shed. Come Monday and his workmate overseer wanted to know if he'd bought the ute. Max said, 'No' and didn't say anything more. It wasn't until sometime later that the ute was discovered in the shed.

Max and Rosemary were married in 1962 and in late 1963, with Stephen on the way, they decided to sell the FB to accommodate the new family member.

Since then Max has had a multitude of vehicles: Zephyr 6 sedan, EH wagon, HR sedan, HT Kingswood sedan, HG Monaro, Toyota Crown sedan, HQ Kingswood, HJ Premier sedan, two Peugeot 504s, Honda Accord, Citroen L-15, FB ute, ZF Fairlane, Datsun 1200 ute, Datsun 120Y sedan, 1923 Peugeot, 1925 Fiat 501 tourer, 1923 T-Model Ford, HG panel van, two Honda Civics, Honda Accord, Nissan Patrol, Nissan Navara ute, FJ sedan and another FB ute.

When Max was working in the Mallee, he often camped out or stayed in the single men's quarters on properties. It was there he fell in love with the FJ Holden ute.

Max had been driving for a Golden Fleece fuel supplier for four years when he was offered a chance to become an AMP insurance agent. For the next 19 years he was a rep all over the country.

Due to skin problems Max needed a change in life, so for the last 10 years he has been working outdoors as a self-employed handyman. He also has a young bloke working with him.

'The FJ ute is my dream – the ultimate, I'm VERY interested in buying one.'

Max's other ute is now his daily work vehicle; a Nissan Navara. 'It's marvellous.' He has racks on the top to carry six-metre ladders. 'Shame they went out of the WB,' says Max. He reckons they were the best.

'In 1980 I bought a Datsun 1200 ute. I was selling insurance out of Mildura and saw it at a railway house in Ouyen with the front corner knocked off it. The owner didn't want to sell it. I saw it again later in Mildura with no motor in it. I ended up buying it for $1200, slipped a motor in it,

re-sprayed and re-upholstered it, and drove it around for a couple of years. My son, Stephen, was learning to drive at the time, and he drove it for a couple of years, too. It was a marvellous little ute – they're so tough.'

Stephen (now 37) is a nurse; Hayley (35), a school principal, Damian (33), a financial planner, and Joel (21), is studying the film industry at college.

'In 1988 I spotted a clean FB ute in Bacchus Marsh. I made enquiries and found out it belonged to a panel-beater bloke at the panel works. I asked if he wanted to sell it and yes, he would, for $3500 including a RWC [*Roadworthy Certificate*].'

It was a quick purchase and Max was amazed at how clean the ute really was. It had a blemish on a front guard and it had been repainted. Max got all the details of its history from the paperwork, and found it had been bought brand new by Clarrie Knight, a builder from Ashwood.

'I tracked down Clarrie Knight's son, Len, who gave me all its original papers and told me more about it. Clarrie had bought it new from Queensbridge Motors. **It looked like it was used only to collect the lunch pies for the men who worked**

for his father's business, **CL Knight &
Sons.** When his father died, Len took over
the ute and continued to use it in the business but finally traded it in on a Mitsubishi
L300 van.

'According to the original papers Len
gave me, his father had bought the ute for
£1116.15.4 including a deluxe windshield,
sunshade, mascot on the bonnet, front
and rear mudflaps, a Diamond Dot push
button radio and turn signal lights.'

Max's own records show that his original
FB ute, without the extras, had cost
£1070. So Clarrie Knight had paid £99.5.9
for all the extras.

When it was sold on 29 October 1985, it
went to Melbourne Auto Auctions, then to
Wheels Plus Car Yard in Footscray, to Barry
Woods in Melton, to Arnold Till on 4 June
1988 and then onto Michael Bone who
owned it for three days and sold it on 30
July 1988 to Max. He won't sell it.

'Actually, I nearly did sell it in 1999, I
even had the roadworthy done. Then I
thought, "No, this is too nice, better
not" and so I kept it and I'm glad I did. I
fell in love with it all over again and now
I hope never to sell it.'

Max has done a bit of
work on the FB over the
years. He used it as his
daily workhorse for many
years and it certainly was
used. He finally re-bored
the motor in about 1993,
re-sprayed the duco and
did a general tidy-up of
the vehicle. 'I bought it
originally because I liked
the look of it. I had a soft
spot because I had owned
one before and it was
very clean-looking when I
bought it.'

The ute continues to be
kept clean and it has been very good for
business – everyone still knows him
because of the FB, even though he now
uses a Nissan Navara ute for work. Max has
a complete list of everything that has ever
been done to the FB. He is very methodi-
cal and keeps all his vehicles in top condition; the Nissan 4WD wagon looks brand
new.

'My dream now is to own a good FJ ute.
I'm still looking. I bought the FJ sedan I
now have, as is. I knocked on the door of

the house where I was told it was for sale.
The man lifted the garage door and as
soon as I saw it, I said, "That's it" and I
bought it on the spot.' The FJ is in perfect
condition, absolutely immaculate. Max got
it for $10 000.

Max doesn't mess around when it comes
to buying vehicles.

'I'm an impulse buyer. I haven't been
far wrong yet, though. You usually have
a fair idea of what you want.'

The Mongrel

I went to my major sponsor and said, 'I want to build a special ute.'

TO CUT A LONG STORY SHORT, I put in a written submission detailing what I envisaged.

I wanted a ute that people would look at from 100 yards away and say, 'Must have a closer look at that.' I wanted to take a standard, everyday production model Ford Falcon AUII and play with it. It had to look as if it could drive across the Gibson Desert! It had to look like it had a bit of muscle - a MONGREL.

I wanted to make the interior into a state-of-the-art 'office'. I spend most of the year on the road writing books, articles for magazines, judging ute shows, etc. This ute had to take the place of my office at home.

Six weeks later we registered the 'MONGREL'. Normally, it would take six to eight months to put a project like this together. I needed to do it in time to take it to the Deniliquin Ute Muster and then to Queensland to the Emerald Ute Muster.

This was a team effort!

I had to get some company sponsors excited about the project. Everyone at Ford was already excited and working beyond the call of duty. I annoyed the hell out of them, probably!

The MONGREL is based on the highly successful AUII Falcon ute, which has already established itself as the market leader in sales and also in terms of ride, handling, power, refinement and comfort. This was something I could really get my teeth into.

The MONGREL is a joint promotional vehicle between Ford and 'The Uteman', in

part of the development. Finally, a couple of days before the ute was ready, I mentioned the name at Ford and that was it.

For me there was a good reason why the name applied. 'Mongrel' described the look we were trying to achieve - something with muscle, rough but tough, individual and special. You always fall in love with mongrel dogs and hopefully, people would feel the same way about the ute. Also though, I have a lifelong mate called 'Mongrel'. I wanted to name the ute in recognition of him and his 90-year-old father. Between them they have owned just about every Ford ute available. Also, a relation of theirs has worked at Ford for many years and I thought the name was an appropriate recognition of Ford loyalty. *[You can read about Mongrel, the man, in my book* Beaut Utes.*]*

My logo reads 'Working for the Bush' and this ute will be used in promotional work in the bush all over Australia.

The MONGREL attracts a lot of attention wherever she goes and she travels many kilometres across this wide land. I have met some really great Aussies because of the MONGREL.

conjunction with a number of aftermarket suppliers of readily available components.

OK. We got it on the road - and did it in amazing time. All contributors are to be congratulated. It was an instant success and has gone on to feature in many motoring magazines and newspaper articles all over Australia.

How did it come to get the name MONGREL? We threw a lot of names around and many suggestions from The Uteman website (uteman.com.au) were considered as

Vehicle Features

Under the bonnet

- Initially, a high output 4.0lt Intech 6 cylinder OHC engine.
  Recently upgraded to a special purring V8, a full exhaust system with a bit of 'bark'
- 5-speed manual transmission
- Anti-lock brakes (ABS)
- Limited slip diff
- Push button traction control
- Power windows
- Smartshield remote central locking
- Electric remote exterior mirrors
- Hi-Series (Fairmont Ghia) instrument panel with automatic climate control, speed alarm. Other work continues.

Interior *(additions so far)*

- Marigold and Warm Charcoal leather trim
- Television tuner/screen, 6 stacker CD changer, speakers
- In-car Nokia 7110 WAP mobile phone
- Dell laptop computer
- UHF radio/receiver

  Still to be added - Satphone, Sat Navigation, DVD, fridge/freezer
  Thanks to Veh-Quip Australia, Clarion Australia, Dell Computers and Optus

Exterior

- Suspension modifications
- Airtec snorkel
- Python 17" x 8" 1 piece polished alloy wheels
- Wrangler F1 235/65R17 tyres
- 6 driving lights
- Polished alloy side bars
- 4-inch rollbar
- Split Tufflid Tonneau
- Special built trailer (built previously)
- Tuff Tonneaus 'Uteman' ute tent
- Trailer Tufflid with computer image, (original artwork). First time that this has been done on a ute in Australia.
- JA45 Dulux autocolour (Yellow) (nicknamed 'Uteman Yella')
- Bodywork by Campbell Smash Repairs
- Bullbar - special one-off airbag compatible

Thanks to TJM Products Australia, Tuff Tonneaus, American Racing Wheels, Goodyear, Veh-Quip, Bluey's Ute World, PPG Australia

Memories of utes

HE DOESN'T OWN A UTE; IN FACT the last one he drove was a work vehicle during the late '80s. The last one he actually owned was a 1930 Chrysler ute - and his mates had to teach him how to drive it home, AFTER he had bought it!

So why is he in a book on utes?

Peter Griffiths has had an exciting time with utes and a great life in general. How many people can say they once owned a ute that went to the top of Australia? The top of the mountain that is - Mount Kosciusko.

He wrote to me about his ute and included a couple of photos. As soon as I saw them, I knew I had to meet him. It meant a long drive interstate to see him in the Australian Capital Territory, but that was OK; I just sensed it would be worth it. So off I went and I'm glad I did.

Peter Griffiths could have a book written about his life. He has lived 71 years to the full so far. Not only has he meticulously made notes of his early outback and mountain travels, but he also has the photos to prove it. He graciously consented to sharing them with everyone. Some are reproduced here. Hopefully, these snippets of Peter's life will entice him to write his autobiography - there is simply not enough space here.

I was honoured to share a full day with Peter and his wife of 46 years, Elaine, at their home where we consumed countless cuppas and a beautiful lunch using antique silverware! (That beats a pie and sauce on the road any day.) The couple's beautiful home and garden backs onto a large lake - a delightful setting - but it was their story and photo albums that had brought me to them.

Peter was adventurous long before they met, and long before anyone had heard of the Leyland Brothers. He first went camping in a cave with some mates when he was about 10 years old and has never lost his love of the bush. His father was a piano tuner and Peter became a piano mechanic when just 15 years old. Then at 18 he became a roof-tiler for 22 years and ended up as a supervisor all over Sydney.

'The other day I got out my old photo albums and relived some of the great trips I have done in beaut old utes.

For instance, I did a trip in a 1927 Chev ute owned by a mate, Dick Redfern. In 1948, I went with some mates to the summit of Mt Kosciusko.'

Peter has a typed diary called 'The Exploits of the Colonel.' This was the nickname they gave their ute and the diary has daily entries of their trip, with photos:

Sunday 26th December 1948

An early summer's morning saw the results of many months' hard work and preparation. All was ready for the gruelling trip of 920 miles. The four grim-faced youths made last minute inspections before taking up their posi-

tions; Dick and Jack in front, and Peter and Roy settled comfortably in the rear. At 6.52 am the ute slowly moved off and made its way through the still sleeping suburb of Punchbowl.

The diary goes on to show the daily life of the adventuring mates, camping and shooting, playing pool at the local pubs en route and many details of the country. One entry shows the test the old Chev ute was put to.

Friday 31st December 1948

At this stage of the journey the 'Colonel' was approaching its first severe test. The much talked of Talbingo Mountain. This mountain road was four miles long and rose to 3900 ft

above sea level. A climb of almost 3000 ft in the four miles. The gallant 'Colonel' negotiated the hill in 35 minutes in low gear all the way and after giving him a spell at the top we proceeded to Yarrangobilly village, which consists of two or three houses with the river of the same name going through.

Numerous other adventures awaited the lads, but finally the entry reaching the top of the mountain is recorded.

Monday 3rd January 1949

An hour later saw us at Hotel Kosciusko. From here the road narrowed and became very uneven and in places very soft and boggy, but without the extra load the road was no match for the 'Colonel' who went along in fine style... Presently Kosciusko loomed in sight but, as a huge snow-drift blocked the road, we were forced to stop some 500 yards from the summit. With wild yells of excitement we clambered headlong up the mountain to the gleaming belt of snow above us ... snowballs flew thick and fast ... standing on top of the mound the wind was so strong that it took us all our strength to hang on.

At last we had reached our objective and it seemed almost unbelievable to think we were now standing on the highest peak in Australia, and at an altitude of 7305 ft above sea level ... It is interesting to note that Jack's 'Nura' cigarette lighter lit at an altitude of 7305 ft - a truly remarkable performance.'

Finally heading off the mountain after making snowmen, a touch of the dramatic is added:

Had we not had our bottle of Bonnington's Irish Moss [cough mixture] we might never have returned to tell of our experiences in the snowy wastes of Kosciusko. We reached Jindabyne around 3 pm and staggered into the tea rooms to be revived by a cold salad and ice cream.'

They were only halfway into their 920-mile trip of 13 days and already many other interesting details fill Peter's diary.

Dick Redfern
Owner, skipper

Jack Redfern
Chief Engineer

Roy Gamble
Navigator

Peter Griffiths
Photographer, Trip Diarist

Of special interest are the picture postcards Peter sent home with little notes like:

Dear Mum,
Everything going fine, living like kings. Went to top of Kossy and played in snow, built snowman.
See you soon. Love to all, Peter.

Eventually the boys and the 'Colonel' reached home safely after many more adventures. It was but one of their trips. Roy and Peter had grown up as little kids together and they met Dick when all three joined the 'Red Cross Younger Set'. Peter was about 15 at the time. All these many years later, they still meet once a year for a reunion. Peter is 71, Roy Gamble is now 73 and Dick Redfern is 74. That's what mateship is all about.

'In 1949, the year of the great coal strike when many of us were out of work, we packed up the old Chev once again and headed for the bush. We got a job sucker cutting and were camped right out in the bush on a property near Merrygoen, near Dubbo. We shared a cabin in the bush near the 600 acres we had to clear.

'We couldn't have been in a better vehicle, as the old Chev was a great stump jumper.

'We also did a lot of pig shooting, but my favourite trip was in my 1929 Dodge when we went prospecting for gold.'

Another of the utes in Peter's life was his own, nicknamed 'Old Parsa', short for 'parsimonious' - a word often used by a roof tiling workmate that means 'stingy' or 'mean'. Every time they had a puncture, his mate, Stan, would yell out, 'You parsimonious old bastard!'

Eventually it was just called 'Old Parsa'.

'I bought it in 1951, but didn't know how to drive, so my mates had to fix up the motor and teach me to drive. I was just 21 and I bought it to do a long Outback trip.'

They had many outback adventures, travelling some 5000 miles, but sadly there is not enough room to relate them here. (Peter's Outback stories will be told in another book by The Uteman.) One thing Peter does say, though, about Outback travel is:

'Don't just dream about it, get yourself a ute and – DO IT!'

In 1955 Peter saw a young lady at a dance and said to his mate, 'Get a load of the blonde'. That lady became his wife, Elaine, and now, 46 years later, they are still mates. They have two children – Michael and Donna – and six grandchildren.

'Back when we first married we only had enough money to buy a block of land, so we went on our honeymoon in an old 1929 Dodge. For two years while we built the

My First Ute

'Dad nearly had a fit when I brought it home – all shiny and the caryard had even painted the tyres so they looked like new. So they were a bit low on tread but they looked good and I couldn't understand what Dad was on about.

'Look, it's an old Holden, yeah, nearly 28 years old, so you've got to expect a bit of rust. Bog? What's bog? Dad, what do you mean it's full of it?

'Well, yeah, I did know about the faulty tail-light and the exhaust bracket, but I'll fix it. No Dad, I didn't know there was wire holding the exhaust on.

'But hey, did you see the beaut radio? Even got subwoofers, listen. Well, gees, it worked real well at the caryard, wire must have worked loose. No worries, Dad, I'll work on it.

'Aw, c'mon, Dad – "used" maybe, but not "a heap of shit". Yeah, I know it needs a paint job. And yes, the seats do need a bit of new upholstery and no, I didn't know about the missing seat belt.

'Aren't the mag wheels great, Dad? They're just the best! The salesman said they were made in a place called Korea. No, they are not worth more than the car.

'Say, did you see it's got a cigarette lighter? No, OK, I don't smoke, but Kylie-Ann does. Yeah, well we might get back together, Dad. If that bloody Martin would piss off, we'd be right. Moron, yeah, I know he is, Dad. What was that, Dad? I couldn't quite hear you.

'And what about those twin exhausts? Listen when I start it up. What's that, Dad? Well, hang on a minute – it might just be a battery terminal. Lift the bonnet. It must be stuck. Yeah, just hold it up, Dad. I don't know where the thingo is that holds the bonnet up.

'OK, here we go then. Oops sorry, Dad. I didn't hit the horn, it just started itself. How's your head? Aw Dad, Mum wouldn't like that sort of language. OK, I'll shut the @#$% up, Dad.

'**Listen at the back to the note on the exhausts. Dad, what are you coughing for? I don't know what the blue smoke means. It isn't too bad, is it?**

'Um, aw, before I forget, the salesman said he'd throw in the plastic mudflaps. They are in the rear - just lift the tonneau. Ah, don't worry, Dad, we can fix that.

Mum's sewing machine should fix the rip, it's only canvas, isn't it?

'What rust? Well, I didn't lift the tonneau. The salesman said the tray was like new so no need to even check. He put the mudflaps in there. Well, he bloody said he'd put them in there. No, I don't frigging well know where the spare tyre is, Dad!

'**Sorry, Dad. It's mine and I like it. Well, I'll own it in six years according to the salesman; he worked it all out. What? Oh, about 20 something per cent, I think. It's on the contract. Well, he kept it; says it'd be on file if I ever needed it.**

'No, I paid a deposit. Just $3137. I signed for it and he gave me the keys. They washed it and put 10 bucks worth of petrol in it. No, I paid him cash, drew all the money out of my bank and put the rest on credit. Um, well, $137 from my savings account and Mum lent me $3000; she said she found it in a tin-box in the garage.

'You alright, Dad? The rest is on credit. Um, $12 999.

'Dad? Dad? You alright, Dad?

'Mum! Muuuuum! Dad's crook. Mum! Dad's lying on the grass.

'MUM!'

Outback Cruiser

SOMETIMES I DON'T HAVE TIME TO DO AN interview with a ute owner on the spot, so I catch up with that person later on. I first met Jonathon Oliver at Wentworth and then some months later outback at Broken Hill, where he has lived most of his life.

I caught up again with him months later when he was fishing in the middle of the Murray River about 10 minutes out of Wentworth. He was in a boat with his uncle. The fish weren't biting either, so it was a good time to yarn.

'It was my very first vehicle. I didn't even have a licence when I bought it at 16, back in 1992. A roo shooter called Kerry Clark from Menindee owned it. It had done 111 000 kilometres and was in reasonable condition; bodywork a bit rough, but it had no rust.'

It was totally stripped down to a chassis sitting on drums. Two years later it had been rebuilt and resprayed and looked new. It had power steering from a 2984 Landcruiser wagon, and a standard motor until 1998 when a 253 V8 was dropped in and air-lockers were put on the diffs.

Since then a five-litre, fuel injected V8 from a VN Commodore Calais has replaced the 253. They found the VN at a wrecker's yard and built a new rear tray that holds four batteries underneath. The cruiser also has two alternators – one 12-volt and the other a 24-volt.

Inside it has Aerotek racing seats, a UHF, a HF with CB, CD player, Rally tripmeter, GPS system and a laptop will be added shortly. Jonathon has also added a top shelf and a dash shelf, as the cruisers normally don't have them.

Checker plate is used extensively throughout – as door trim, and as a centre consol that has also been fitted with a transmission oil temperature gauge. Of course, it has a mobile phone. There's a 24-volt electric winch and a snorkel.

Lighting is well provided for with a roof-mounted spotlight for shooting, two lights for reversing, four spotlights on the roof and three on the rollbar. Something tells me this thing lights up pretty well in the dark around Broken Hill.

Jonathon is a third year motor mechanic in Broken Hill. Dad, Dennis and his wife, Julie, own the Silver City 4WD Centre in Broken Hill. Jonathon's stepbrother, Wayne, is 32, and another, Kim, very sadly died a couple of years ago, aged 27, in a car accident in Adelaide.

'Dad and I worked on nearly all of the ute rebuild together. So far we've spent about $70 000 on it. I'll never sell it.'

'It was called "Battlestar Gallatica" by my mates because of its size and all the aerials I used to have on it. I don't know what I'd do without a ute – they really are an icon.

'**Dad reckons it is just a bit of a boy's toy.**'

One-legged Woodcutter, 3 Gravediggers & the White Ghost

They breed them tough in the Llewellyn family.

MICK LLEWELLYN WORKED INTO HIS 90s, cutting wood all his life and died when he was nearly 102 years old. His son, Syd, won the first wood-chopping contest he ever entered - aged 14. He had an accident in the forest when he was 24 and lost one leg and nearly the other but within a few months he was back working.

Three generations of the family have also been gravediggers. Syd's father dug graves by hand for 27 years. Sixty-seven-year-old Syd is still doing it after 40 years, and his eldest son, Tony, for the last 14 years.

'That's how the ute got the name the "White Ghost". I'd been finishing off digging a grave somewhere just on dark and someone who knew me said they'd seen the "White Ghost" at the cemetery. Anyone and everyone around the district knows it by that name now.'

Syd seems pretty proud of the fact that his father lived so long.

'Dad left school at 11 and took off up to Deniliquin where he was taught to be a shearer by a bloke called Billy Snowden, and we have photos of Dad when he was carting wool on wagons pulled by bullocks. He later had a horse and tip dray. He'd shovel gravel out of the creeks; it was used to make roads. He got paid nine pence for a yard of gravel. For the rest of his life he cut wood, dug graves and we had stock trucks as well.

'Dad was never over 11 stone in his whole life, but very wiry and tough as old goat's knees. He smoked all his life - Havelock flake roll-your-own tobacco. He didn't know anything else but work. All his life.

'Dad had one ute in his lifetime. A late '60s International. He used it for carting wood. One day he came home and the near side of the ute had a couple of white marks on it. I asked what he'd hit and he said he'd brushed a couple of white posts. He said, "That's it. I'm selling the ute and going to give the licence away." He was well into his 80s. I asked if his eyesight had failed and he said, "It's gone to buggery".

'Dad broke his hip when he was 100. They operated and pinned it. I used to visit him in hospital, shave him and make a tin of fags for him. Anyway, I pushed him out in the wheelchair to sit outside. He said to me, "Better make me another cigarette", which I did and he smoked it. When he finished he said, "Well, that's it lad, that's my last one, I'm finished". I said, "Don't worry, Dad, you'll see a few more white shirts yet". He replied, "No, a couple more days and I'll be finished". That was the Friday and he died on the Sunday just as I was leaving home to go and see him.

'He used to donate wood to the hospital every year and they made him a life governor of the hospital in 1927. We buried him in the local cemetery and he always said I had to dig his grave, so I kept my promise to him.'

Like his father before him, Syd Llewellyn took to cutting wood when he was young. He left school at 14 and with another bloke he began contract cutting for the boilers at a local goldmine. Fifteen shillings for a ton of wood. With his Blitz truck and block and tackle, he also helped to hoist the huge timbers to construct the poppet legs. It still stands there today.

He then joined his father and they worked together for nearly all of the next 25 years. His father had a tray truck and Syd a semi and they carted stock to the markets.

Syd has cut wood since 1949 and 52 years later in 2001, he is still at it. He says he is a slowing down a bit. He only cuts about 300 ton a year now!

His long working life in the bush started with an axe, then progressed to crosscut saws, dragsaws, swingsaws and finally to chainsaws. He still has five Stihl chainsaws in the shed. It was the swingsaw that took his leg and nearly his life. It is still in the shed.

'Dad and I were cutting and he was on the swingsaw and I was nearby. A large branch fell, kicked up, caught me between the legs and threw me backwards and I landed on the saw. It took one leg completely off at the top. A tobacco tin in my other pocket caught the blade, jammed it and stalled the engine.

'I didn't feel anything. I looked down and blood was pouring out everywhere. I looked up again and saw my leg lying some distance away. Dad didn't panic. He untied the bootlace off the severed leg and tied it around what was left and got a stick and twisted it tight. He then got a rope and tied it around the other leg and made it tight.

'He said he would go for help at a farm a mile away. I said, "Make me a smoke first". I sat there while he ran through the

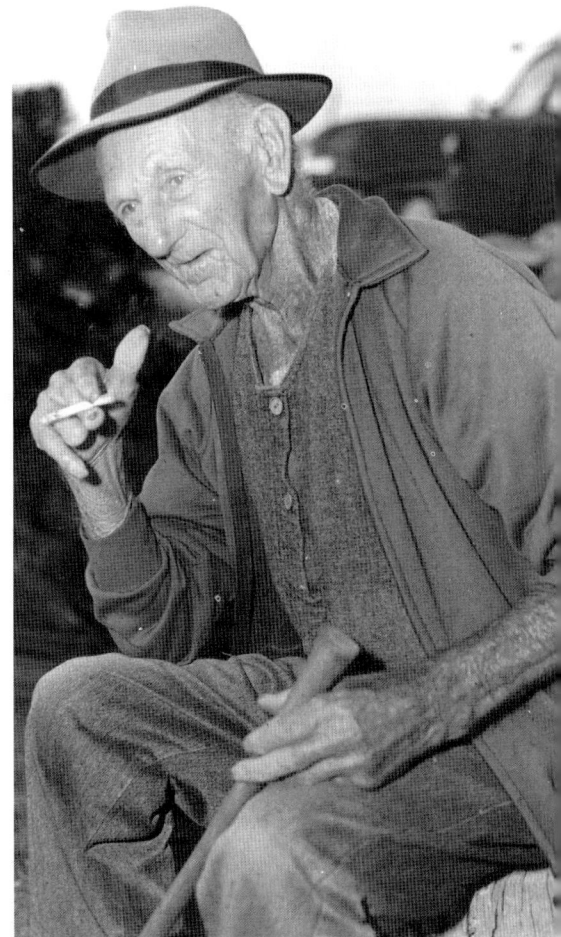

bush. **When the doctor and ambulance got to me I was covered with hundreds of ants that must have smelt the blood. The doctor said that he couldn't administer painkillers because I had lost so much blood. He said, "You'll just have to bear it, Syd".**

'The ride to hospital was the fastest I've ever had in my life. It was then they found out I have a rare blood type. They tried everywhere to get blood and finally got enough to keep me going. It had to be flown in by helicopter. The rest eventually came from South Australia.

'When I was in hospital they had two nurses doing nothing else but pulling ants and sawdust off me. The doctors said if it hadn't been for my father's quick work, I wouldn't have lasted much longer as I'd lost so much blood. I owe him my life.

'I finally got out of hospital and, on crutches, I used to go up to the houses in the street, sit on their back doorsteps and cut kindling wood for their fires. I'd sit there for hours, just so I could do something. **Finally, one day I said to my brother-in-law, "Leave the ute today, I want to go and cut some wood". He said, "How are you going to do that?"** Well,

off I went into the bush. I sat my bum on the ground next to trees and with chainsaw in hand, cut logs into blocks, which were then loaded by my wife.'

The ute is a 1972 Holden Kingswood. It has the original 186 motor. It has been serviced every 1000 miles by the same mechanic, Phil Archer, since the day Syd got it. **It had done 62 000 miles when he bought it and now it's done an extra 300 000 more. It is the only ute he's ever owned.**

'A fella in a town a few miles away bought the ute new and looked after it like we look after our missus.

'Some years later my eldest son, Tony, was looking for a ute and so we bought it. He later wanted a more modern one. He traded it in on a Falcon, but lost his licence. We used to drive him at 3.00 am to a bakery were he worked and often the Falcon had problems starting. One day I did my lolly with him and I said, "I'm not driving that again".

'**I rang the caryard and said, "Do you still have that white Holden ute my son traded in?" Yes, they did, and so I bought it back off them.** All it has had done to it over the years is two or three clutches, wheel bearings and an alternator. The motor and transmission are original.

'**Even though it has been overloaded most of its life, it still goes OK, but it is starting to get the death rattles. I reckon this year might see her out.**

'If you'd seen some of the loads she's carted! If I said she'd carried eight or ten thousand ton of wood on her over the years, I wouldn't be exaggerating. I wouldn't be lying. She's been marvellous.'

The ute has towed a few two-horse floats to the trots over the years, too. Syd has his own trotting horses and has won many races in his time. He's been training horses for over 30 years. 'Great and Small', which has won $82 000 in prize money, is his best horse to date. It still holds a course record on one track - 2.4 for the 2580 metres.

'There's no comparison between these utes and the new ones today. They are tough these older ones; always better, I reckon. I've never had a breakdown in the bush. Bogged - any amount of times!

'**She's been such a bloody good ute to me. I'd hate to sell it. I've got a bit of an eye on getting a 4WD Triton, though. I still want to keep cutting wood.**'

When Syd heard I'd just bought another old ute for my ute museum, he immediately said, 'I'll tell you what I'll do, I won't trade it in, I'll keep it for you for when your museum is ready. I'd like that.'

And Syd, I'd be proud to put your ute and story in the museum. I've always said writing about utes has led me to some of the most interesting people you could meet in your life. Syd Llewellyn is one of them. A tough, hard-working man, but also a bit of a gentleman; friendly and someone who loves a bit of a yarn. Buy wood off him and you'll get more than you paid for. Honesty brings loyal customers.

Syd and wife, Doreen, are life members of the local football club where he was president and she was in charge of running the kiosk. Doreen still does volunteer work in the hospital kiosk.

I helped him load some red gum blocks onto the Holden ute ready to go to a local customer that afternoon. Finally, his wife arrived home from her volunteer work at the hospital and it was time for me to hit the road again.

Syd rolls another cigarette with his strong hands.

We shake hands and again he mentions that he'll keep the ute for when my ute museum opens. I said we'd have to have a load of wood on it because it just wouldn't be the same without it.

He said, 'Don't worry, I reckon I could arrange that!'

I have no doubt he could.

One-Tonner 'JJ'

HE WAS GOING THE OTHER WAY SO I HAD to do a fast U-turn and chase him. I knew I couldn't hold him up for long as his ute gave a pretty good indication of his employment - John Jefferies is a sub-contract courier. I explained who I was on the side of the road and in between cars and trucks whizzing by, I got his contact details and we parted.

The next weekend I travelled to his 140-acre farm to have a closer look at his red 1982 WB one-tonner, and to learn more about him and the ute.

'I've always been a Holden man. I was driving past a second hand caryard and saw it. I pulled over and my then wife asked what I was doing. "I'm going back to buy that ute!" She thought I was joking, but I knew dead-set that it was mine. It was sitting there all red in the sunshine and I just thought - it's mine. A few days later it was, and the Mazda 1800V ute was gone.

'That was about seven years ago. It had 170 000 kilometres on the clock. It now has 600 000 kilometres on it. The original motor was getting a bit tired, so rings and bearings have been done. All I've done is add a CB radio and a bullbar, which has since hit two kangaroos.'

John, or JJ as he is known, sub-contracts for Symes Transport and he delivers everything from car parts and clothing, to paper for printers and anything else that can fit on the ute. His 'territory' is from Bendigo to Gisborne, across to Lancefield and west as far as Maryborough, and any town in between. He travels from 200 to over 1000 kilometres a week. John enjoys the freedom of the open road in his ute.

'I left school at 15 and was a builder and carpenter for 20 years, but then the building trade was in a low so I went and became a gold miner at Wattle Gully mine. I was underground for eight years on jackhammers and other equipment. When it closed I took on driving.'

JJ, 52, is now divorced and lives on his farm, where his father once had trotting horses. His son Steven, 30, works as a service station attendant. He lives at home with JJ, and they share a love of Holden utes. JJ's daughter, Tammy, is 28, single and a secretary.

JJ is no stranger to utes. He first owned a Toyota Hilux, then one of the last model Valiants, then a Mazda 1800 and now the WB Holden.

'I just wouldn't be without one, especially out here on the farm. It's carted wood for the home fires here and we've always towed a caravan on holidays and fishing trips - you just stack all the stuff on the back of the ute. It held me up once in the bush, stuck in reverse gear. The linkages broke, and I had to learn on the spot how to put them right with some wire, then we were OK.'

JJ says he will 'keep it forever' and the lure of the open highway is still with him. Although he has already been around Australia once, he wants to do it again and by the time you read his story, he will be 'somewhere out there'. His dream is to

follow Highway One around the coastlines of Australia, and just see what eventuates for six to 12 months. He plans to put a canopy on the back of the ute, and just tow a 6 x 4 trailer. But the farm will never be sold and will always be home for JJ. Son Steven will look after the place. *[See Steven's story 'EH Freak' on page 49]*

Jessie, the Golden Retriever, now over 10 years old and 'Beanie' the 18-month-old Blue Heeler were pleased to see a new face and loved a final pat from a wandering author of ute books.

orange R/T hemi-charged

'DAD WOULDN'T LET ME BUY AN XF, BUT I knew he liked Valiant Chargers as he'd had them himself, so I kept annoying him until he agreed, and when he saw a photo of the VK Valiant in the magazine, he said, "Right, we are going to have a look at that". So we did and we bought it. I was 16.'

There's more than one way to get your Dad to buy a ute when you're young, and Brendan Condon certainly found one. The ute was owned by a bloke who did up hotrods and he needed some money to finish a project, so he sold his ute to the Condons for $4500. The motor had clocked up 40 000 kilometres since it was rebuilt.

He might have been too young to drive it on the roads at the time, but Brendan had 13 acres of the family property to drive around in until he got his licence. He learnt to drive when he was four or five and always liked utes, especially his mum's XF. Dad had a Dodge that he liked also.

The Valiant is a 1976 VK with a 265 Hemi motor. It was just a plain orange ute with the black stripes but when Brendan got it, and even against his father's wishes, he set to and added a few things. His father changed his mind and now he really likes the look of it.

'It won't be sold. I think Dad really wants it. He had an identically coloured Charger.'

Brendan's father put on a bullbar, side skirts, driving lights, CD player, CB radio and UHF. 'It has power steering and sway bars - it handles really well,' says Brendan.

He turns 19 this year and will go to his first B&S Ball with some of his mates. Needless to say, the VK will be a different sight to the usual Holdens and Fords.

Brendan also has a 1978 Dodge pickup, the same as one his father also owned. It has a 245 Hemi, 4-speed manual, Sunraysias, CB and rollbar. He has had it for six months but now thinks he'll sell it and use that money on something else. He just doesn't need it anymore.

'I've always loved utes.'

As a third year apprentice diesel mechanic, he works mainly on Volvo trucks. The mudflaps on his ute are Volvo truck flaps. 'I cop a lot of shit from my mates about them. They reckon they shouldn't be on there.'

Ute drivers reckon one ute equals a million Volvo cars.

His parents will learn when they read this that the ute has been stacked.

Brendan was in his ute racing a brother on his motorbike up the driveway of their parents' property. Brendan braked and the back-end, being so light, moved sideways - he hit an embankment and bent the bull-bar. Boys will be boys.

When he is finished with the B&S scene, this is a ute that Brendan could make into an excellent-looking street machine. If he ever buys another ute, I'm sure that his Dad will get his hands on the Orange VK, and if not his Dad, then maybe one of his brothers. Gavin is 17, Damian, 16 and Cameron is 14. Utes will continue to play a part in the family.

'You gotta get a ute.'

rachel

'You don't really want to put the ute in the book do you'?

I THINK RACHEL BORG WOULD HAVE preferred I wrote a book on Landcruisers. Her old 1975 Mazda B2000 has been a hard worker and is still going but spends its days in the backyard of her place, the battery hooked up to provide electric fencing that keeps the horses from wandering.

She unhooked the fencing and started the ute. Blue smoke wafted across the yard. She laughed as she backed up and drove it to where I wanted to photograph it. Then she brought her Landcruiser around and parked it in the background. Next, it was a case of rounding up some of her horses and of course, 'Tonny' the adorable dog wasn't going to miss out on

the action, nor were her two cats, 'Hooch' and 'Indiana'.

'The ute was bought off a mate for $1000. He had used it as a farm ute, mainly to collect firewood in. It has also been used as a daily work ute carrying building tools and materials; often overloaded.'

Now, apart from providing battery power, it is used to carry hay and all sorts of horse feed, saddles and other gear.

'It's reliable. He's a good ute,' says Rachel. 'He might get a new motor shortly and then I'll probably drive it to work and save on maintenance for the Landcruiser.'

This is Rachel's third ute. She has previously had an XF Ford and a Holden HX 1-tonner. She and partner, Brett, also have a Holden Overlander.

Animals have always played a huge part in Rachel's life. When she was tiny her parents recall that, at the zoo or in the park, Rachel would always run up to the animals. She has always had a fascination for them.

Now 30, she recalls that as a kid growing up, she owned a cat and a dog. She also used to walk up the road and help out at a dairy farm just to be near the ani-

mals. The farmer taught her how to ride a horse. She has also helped out on a Hereford stud.

Rachel wanted to be an agricultural secretary, but ended up working in insurance assessing where she gained an Affiliate Diploma in General Insurance. She has worked for a number of companies, usually for about three years at each. At one time she became personal secretary to an AMP million-dollar salesman, which kept her busy.

Finally, after several years, she was tired of being a secretary and, determined to work with animals and still wanting to get into the science field, she quit a good job.

'I made up my mind. I thought: That's it, I want to do it. I don't care if I get a job, I'll study until I can get in.'

She applied for a job with a university where a friend was working with animals. But with no relevant experience, she missed out. However, the interviewer was impressed – she had already enrolled in the course. Finally, Rachel managed to get to a second interview and was employed. She has been there now for five years and was recently promoted to manager of the animal facility. She completed a Diploma of Applied Science (Animal Technology) part-time over four years and intends to complete further studies after a break.

Rachel knows where she is headed. At the time of writing this story, she and Brett are buying a farm. Her long-term goal is to become a trainer of thoroughbred racehorses. She plans to do a three-year course, get her trainer's licence and turn her farm into a stabling complex. I have no doubt she will achieve her goals.

'**We want the lot - horses, pigs, chooks, dogs, cats. We just love the lifestyle of living in the country and working in the city. I want to stay working at the university with a good career, but always want to have a country life with animals.**'

They both ride their horses and compete in picnic races all over in three states - from the Flinders Ranges, Roxby Downs and other parts of the South Australian outback, to the Victorian High Plains and Merimbula in New South Wales. They have even ridden as far away as Alice Springs.

And what about Rachel's capabilities with horses? She does most things pretty well, as the ribbons and trophies testify. Her latest favourite is 'Kubra' (registered name: 'Tulloch's Diesel and Dust') a one-year-old buckskin leopard Appaloosa colt. 'I chose the name "Kubra" because I wanted something Australian,' she says. After only two months of training, Kubra won a whole heap of awards - 'Colt Two Years and Under' and 'Champion Stallion or Colt' at the summer Royal Melbourne Show. He won the 'One Year and Under

Colt' award at the Victorian State Appaloosa Championships, and also took out 'Reserve Champion Colt'.

Something tells me we are going to hear a lot more of Kubra and Rachel. She has a great way with her animals and she'll have plenty of work with Kubra, an intelligent and cheeky young horse.

Every time I go to visit Rachel and Brett he comes to greet me, but all he wants is to do is chew the tarp off my ute!

'Riddo'

MICHAEL RIDINGS HAS A MUM WHO worked for a stock and station agent, which meant he got the chance to spend time helping out with the stock in the local stockyards.

His father owns an earthmoving company in Bathurst, New South Wales, so 'Riddo' (as everyone knows him) has spent a lot of time on the rural side of life. He took out a trade as a plant mechanic. He always wanted to be a pilot and completed his training in light aircraft. He still holds a private pilot's licence.

'My ute-driving life started when I was just 11. Dad bought me an old Valiant to learn to drive in. It was a six-cylinder auto on the tree, full of rust and no tread left on the tyres, but I learnt to keep control of it and started to turn it into a feral. I put every sticker I could find on it, and taught myself how to do circle work.'

Riddo kept the ute for a few years but sold it for what they had paid for it ($200). His father's old XF work ute became his when he got his 'L' plates. **Shortly after he got his licence, an 89-year-old bloke drove out in front of the ute and caused an accident that saw Riddo's ute written off.**

Next was a 4WD diesel Toyota Hilux which won Best Feral Ute at the 1998 Bathurst races. When Riddo started his apprenticeship at Komatsu, he traded the Hilux in for a 1997 Falcon Longreach GLI. It was an ex-Lithgow Council ute that the dogcatcher had used. It had low kilometres and looked like new.

'I was rapt. I started with a set of my favourite 12-slotter mags that look good on any Falcon, then I bought a nudge bar, skirts, clearance lights, bull-lights, aerials, CB, phone - the works. One day when I was still working at Cadia Mines in Orange, I hit a big roo that smashed the whole front spoiler. The next day I ordered a polished alloy bullbar and a four-and-a-half inch rollbar as well. Since then the ute has had four complete changes of stickers, two tailgates, four sets of rear tyres and two fronts.

'There's been some minor battle damage from going to B&S Balls. I started going to Bachelor and Spinster Balls in 1999. My first was at Monkerai and when I saw all the utes there, I said to myself that I'd be back the next year and win. Since then I have received: a first Best Rural Ute at Monkerai 2000; an Outright Winner at Monkerai 2000; a second in the Best Rural Ute section at Bathurst 2000; a second in Best Rural Ute at Gulgong 2000; a second Best Rural Ute at Woodstock 2000; a nomination for Ute of the Millennium at Deniliquin 2000; and the last award was a first for Best Rural Ute at Tamworth 2001.'

Not bad for a ute that started off as a dogcatcher's daily work vehicle!

It was at the Boorowa B&S Ball 2000 that Riddo met Erin Commins, a 20-year-old dental therapist from Dubbo. They had both been at the Forbes B&S in 1999, but didn't meet. It wasn't until Erin was looking through Riddo's photos that she saw herself and a cousin in the background of a photo of his ute.

'It was just meant to be, and now we do everything possible together. We travel in the ute as much as possible, seeing heaps of countryside. From when we first met at

Boorowa B&S, we have had the closest of relationships that anyone could imagine.'

I hadn't met Erin at the time, but I first met Riddo a couple of years ago at a ute show and B&S. We met again at the Tamworth Ute Show in January 2001, and unbeknownst to anyone, Riddo had a surprise in store.

It was at one of Lee Kernaghan's concerts that Riddo managed to get himself on stage and, before Lee and an enthusiastic crowd, proposed to Erin. The crowd went wild. Lee made the evening by singing *Goondiwindi Moon* to the couple, and presenting them with a bottle of champagne. **The ute is now called Goondiwindi Moon and this is written on the bonnet bug deflector.**

What the crowd didn't know was that Lee also invited the couple to visit him at his hotel the next day for a yarn and a swim in the pool. Lee told me later that it was a pretty special moment for him. It was certainly something the two lovebirds will remember in their old age.

The next morning I met Riddo and introduced him to another of his favourite country singers - Adam Brand. Riddo, of course, soon had another signature to add to the mudguard of his ute. All in all, Tamworth Country Music Festival 2001 was a big highlight for the couple.

Good luck, guys - and may your ute journey through life always be on smooth roads.

Scott, Donna & Middy

SCOTT BROWN AND HIS GIRLFRIEND, Donna, are living proof that there can be more than one ute in the family, and neither are your usual tradesperson or bush-bomb ute drivers.

Scott holds a degree with a double major in economics and commercial law. He is a former road train owner/operator. Donna has a degree in human movement and is now doing a post-graduate degree in health promotion. She represented Western Australia in junior basketball and still plays for East Perth in the State Basketball League.

After he left school, Scott worked driving forklifts whilst doing his university degree. Two years later he bought a Kenworth SAR road train with a 400 CAT and a guarantee of five year's work driving Esperance-Perth-Esperance. Later, he drove six nights a week from Perth to Lake Grace and back again. In 18 months he clocked up 320 000 kilometres. In early 2000 he sold his business, but drove for another company until he found his present job.

Scott's first ute was a HJ Holden - a one owner original with three on the tree and a 202 motor. The old man who had owned it did 130 000 kilometres in 17 years and only carried one load of sand in it. Scott added mags, a rollbar and, against his father's wishes, a 253 V8, a new gearbox and diff. He spent $6000 in 12 months. It was then lowered and repainted - another $3500.

Scott had just got it back from rebuilding. His grandfather died on the Friday of that week. He turned 21 on the Sunday and at his grandfather's funeral on the Tuesday, he pulled out from the cemetery, straight into another car and did $4000

worth of damage. The police nailed him for failing to give way and Scott lost his licence the following week.

The ute was repaired and a Statesman grille and a bullbar were added. Finally it was sold in May 2000, with Scott having spent some $35 000 to get it to the way he wanted it. It was time to move on and move into a new ute.

Scott's present ute is a Bermuda blue, five-litre 1998 Holden VS ute, which he bought when it had done 35 000 kilometres but it 'came with all the fruit,' as Scott says. 'A CD player, ROH wheels, three-inch big bore exhaust, rollbar and nudge bar.' Scott has since added polished alloy side skirts and a UHF.

Both Scott and Donna drive their own 'special' utes.

Donna is ute mad in general, but particularly keen on her first and only vehicle –

a restored 1964 EH Holden ute called 'Ernie'. A local Katanning 16-year-old originally restored it. It was rebuilt from three different utes. Now it has a 186 red motor, M21 gearbox, SAAS racing seats, dragway five-spoke mag wheels, polished alloy side skirts, an EJ dash and tail-lights.

The other part of the family is their two-year-old Blue Heeler dog called 'Middy' – named because she was born at midday. 'Middy is very loyal and highly disobedient,' says Scott. 'She is unstoppable; she likes to bite the pressure cleaner which runs at 1600 psi, while you are washing the truck. She loves the ute and will sleep in the back all day just to make sure you do not leave without her.'

Both Scott, 24, and Donna, 21, have grown up and lived in many country towns in Western Australia. Although now based in Perth, they like nothing better than heading bush when time permits to go to B&S Balls, to go wakeboarding, and to help mates with seeding on farms - as they do each year.

Scott now works for the Department of Productivity and Labour Relations (DOPLAR), but still finds time to drive trucks at weekends.

Some weekends he might leave Perth on a Friday, working two trips Perth-Port Hedland-Karratha-Perth, two up. He arrives home Sunday morning. Another trip he often does is Perth to Ceduna in South Australia and back to Perth. He arrives home 4500 kilometres later on Sunday night - ready to start another week in the office on Monday morning.

There's one thing for sure; this young, vibrant couple will have their special utes for a long time, and Middy the Blue Heeler will remain a happy girl for a long time to come, too.

The Stoneman

HE'S THE 'STONEMAN' AND THEY have been called 'Mr and Mrs Rock', and no wonder, as Dave and Kathy McDonald know a fair bit about stone and rock. They carted stone and slate to build their own home and Dave has gone on to make his mark in this world in a way that will be around long after he's gone.

He has built many stone homes, garages, dry stone walls, fences, paths, ornamental gardens, chimneys and more. He has diversified into stone carving, making a variety of excellent sundials, water fountains and gargoyle statues – all out of a wide range of bluestone, granite, sandstone and slate.

'Once you start with stone, you just never stop, you always fiddle with it.'

Dave has always been pretty good with his hands; he has made all sorts of timber furniture, and was also a welder. When a friend built a stone shack, he and Kathy fell in love with it. They wanted a cheap home to build, so they started mucking about with stone, and with Kathy's brother, began to build two homes - one for the brother and one for themselves. They had a 90-acre block of land in a valley of natural bush, and so they knew their future would be here.

I asked Kathy about stone.

'We used to go out collecting rocks in the bush - it was great fun. Our old ute went through hell, but it was a tough old ute.'

Dave had been building concrete water tanks at the time, and he got a 'bit of a name' as a stone builder as time went on. He is basically self-taught - he did a weekend course, talked to a lot of old guys, read all he could and was building full-

time for about 11 years. 'I'm still learning, even now,' he says.

They showed me their photo albums and Dave can be mighty proud of his achievements. Believe it or not, after all that time and the thousands of tons of stone he's moved - sometimes as high as three stories onto buildings - his back is still OK. However, he was getting tired, he says.

'I was out everywhere building other people's dreams. I figured it was time for mine, so I changed.

'It took me nearly two years to get out of the business, to wind up all the work I had booked ahead. If someone came along tomorrow and gave me a real challenge, like building a castle with all the gargoyles and stuff, I'd be off like a shot. I'd have more labour-saving devices now, though.'

And so four years ago Dave changed direction. He had a Diploma of Visual Arts and was into stone carving and saw a new possibility. He's now four years into a Bachelor of Visuals Arts degree with one year to go. He wants to set up a future direction for the family, hopefully doing some teaching and working from home creating his own business identity. He has been selling sundials and other stone carv-

ings through a shop. This is an expanding interest. (I ordered a unique sundial for my own garden.) Sculpturing is his passion.

'I just simply wanted to improve,' he says matter-of-factly. Kathy adds, 'University has certainly brought out the talent he has.'

'Basically, I've never been without a ute,' says Dave. When I got my licence I had a red 1976 VH Dodge which went everywhere for 12 to 15 years. I was working with my father who is an apiarist. We chased bees all over the country for years.

'The second ute was also a Dodge. I drove it for a while, but it was a bit rough so I fixed it up, painted it undercoat grey, then resprayed it and sold it. We were at my brother's place, and there was a Dodge in the shed with one day of registration left on it. He gave it to us and we drove it home from Byron Bay.

'Then I had a Nissan Patrol ute which was going to be done up, but never was, so it's a paddock basher now. The Daihatsu was just a big ute (two-and-a-half tonne) and we used it to carry stone, slate and anything else that was heavy. It's still sits up the hill in the bush. She wore out too. The Landrover is now used around the paddocks and for wood-carting, stone-carrying, etc. Needs a few things done to it. Originally, I bought it off my Dad.

'Very hard life that one - carrying stuff for stonework. It's been overloaded most of its life!'

The Landrover is now very soft in the springs and needs some attention. It has done lots of hard miles. Dave reckons it's great to work off the back of, but he'd like to put a flat-top tray on it. It was one of the best when he got it. It has an Isuzu diesel in it, which has never had a spanner on it but it's heavy on fuel, though. He says if you put it in 4WD low range, it'll climb anything.

And so the Stoneman continues to study and it won't be long before he'll get back

out there with stone on the ute, to build his dreams. His talent is expanding and he has many people wanting him to do work for them.

Don't forget, I ordered that special sun-dial for the garden, Stoneman.

But the last word is Kathy's; she jumped in quick when I asked her what she thought of utes.

'Can't live without them!'

True. Once you've had a ute, life is never the same.

The Stout

IT WAS SITTING IN A MAIN STREET OF A large country town as I drove past and of course, it caught my eye, so I went back. The owner wasn't around, so I wrote a note on the back of my business card and went to put it on the windscreen. As I did so, two blokes came around the corner and walked towards the ute.

They were in a hurry - big time - but graciously consented to driving around the corner away from all the other parked vehicles to let me get a couple of photos.

As we were talking, a hot Holden ute drove past up the hill, did a U-turn and parked in front of my ute. A young bloke got out and started checking my ute over. We ute drivers are like that - we always like to have a chat with another ute driver and compare utes.

The two blokes I met first had an appointment to get to and a long drive ahead, so I shook hands with owner, David Munro, and his mate, Alan Ackroyd, and we parted company. I rang David at home near Newcastle later and we discussed his rather unusual ute.

David is a prospector and spends a lot of time in the bush. He had a Type 3 VW converted for bush work, but decided to get a new vehicle. He and his mate, Tony, were looking through a caryard and there, tucked away up the back of the yard amongst a heap of other vehicles, was the 1977 Toyota Stout, with canopy.

Tony said 'That's you down to a T, mate.'

'You reckon?' replied David.

'Anyway, we took it for a test drive. It went well. It was slow and just a bit basic. It has a two-litre motor, and four on the column. It is a bit light in the tray. For my work in the bush, you don't want anything too flash, vehicles get scratched.

'It really is "bush worthy" and you need a tough vehicle. I think from memory I paid about $1100 for it. In fact, I didn't really realise what I had bought until it was sitting outside my place in the street. It was then that I could see it was a big chucky vehicle - it sort of got swamped amongst all the other vehicles in the caryard.'

David is the first to admit it is not a road vehicle. It is a bit slow and uncomfortable. On one trip he blew the exhaust and a timing case seal. Other than that it has been mechanically good. On the highways it averages 80 to 85 kph.

'I am not sure of its history, but it looks like it may have been used as a farm vehicle and for spotlight shooting. There are attachments for spotlights all over it.

'It is good for what I have been doing as a prospector, as I cover a lot of miles in the bush. It is good for carting things around on, and I'll keep it for a long while yet.'

In all my travels around looking at utes, I've seen and written about Stouts, but this is the first time I have come across one with a full styleside box-type tray. All others have been flat-top trays. Obviously, there aren't as many around now.

He told me that when he was getting petrol this morning a bloke came up to him and commented on his unusual ute.

I'm sure other ute lovers will also appreciate David sharing details of his special ute.

Sexy Lindy May

Will I or won't I? Yeah, I have to see it up close.

SO IT WAS YET ANOTHER U-TURN AND chase through the suburbs until he finally pulled into a large warehouse. I knew he would, it had 'courier' written on the side of the door, so I figured he was either doing a delivery or going back to base.

David Risojevic knew I was following him. He said to his mate beside him, 'This bloke is following me'. He was right; I was. I didn't want to hold him up from his work so I took some photos and let him get back to it. We spoke later that day when he had finished work.

'It's a 1985 Toyota HJ75 Landcruiser. I bought it off a Mrs Ennis. Her husband, Bluey, had died and it was advertised in the car classifieds. He was the original owner and used it to tow a trailer loaded with firewood. It was 'stock as a rock' with 140 000 kilometres on it.'

David has a get-up-and-go attitude. At only 25, he has worked as a jackaroo on Rosewood station in the Northern Territory and has also had an alloy-polishing business; the cruiser was his on-site service unit. He polished the alloy on big trucking rigs at transport companies. Now as a sub-contractor, he is on the road all over, averaging 3000 kilometres a week.

'She has a 2H four litre diesel motor but no turbo, a CB, a UHF, a two-way radio back to the work office, scanner, six stack CD player, custom trim inside, a 12 volt TV, a driver's seat from an ambulance and she will soon have a DVD player for when we go camping. I designed the tray. I knew exactly what I wanted.

'We even used the Landcruiser ute as our wedding car.'

And what does his wife, Melinda, think of the ute?

'I love it; no way known is he going to sell it. It's unique, something different, one of a kind. I'm not usually into cars, but he will sell it over my dead body,' she laughs.

'Sometimes I'd like to blow the ute up, he spends so much time looking after it,' laugh Melinda. 'It's his baby.'

David services the ute every two or three weeks. Every week it gets a full grease change on everything that moves. He takes it off-road about every four months, just to get oil through the gears and diffs, but never gets too carried away in the bush. He just takes it easy and makes sure it runs well.

He says that with the alloy he tries to keep on it all the time, it needs to be completely polished every two weeks, and in addition, the ute is washed every third day. Not surprisingly, this ute has won some trophies in shows such as Best Work Ute and Best Custom Ute.

It is not David's first ute, though. That was a Datsun 720 ute with a bug deflector that read 'Bull Breaker' on it. Then he got into the B&S Ball scene with his mates. He had an 81 WB ute with bullbar, rollbar and the works, including a bug deflector that said 'Riding for a Fall'.

'But then I hung up my spurs. Now I have a beautiful wife and a baby on the way. I got responsible and settled down to build a future.'

They still go to the country at weekends and meet up with mates now and then, but the dog, 'Ebony', and cat, 'Snoopy', now take pride of place. Something tells me David had better get used to a different kind of baby; the one about to arrive doesn't come with a lot of chrome – only dirty nappies. He seems pretty excited about it all, though.

He has a business attitude bound to succeed: 'Big enough to serve, but small enough to care.'

'There's no point in sitting on your arse waiting for things to happen; just get off it and have a go. And as for the ute, it will be rotting in the backyard before it is ever sold.' Somehow, I can't ever see that happening.

Stuchbery Bros.

ALTHOUGH THEY ARE BROTHERS, DAVID and Ray Stuchbery are like chalk and cheese: one is a quiet gentleman, the other a loud larrikin. Ray, alias 'Blue the Bush Larrikin' had his story in *More Beaut Utes*.

David's ute is clean, very standard and well looked after. Ray's is untidy, a bit of a bomb and never looked after. David is just your normal nice sort of a bloke, unassuming – and very talented. Blue is full on, in ya face and, as his nickname suggests, a bit of a bush character. He also is very talented.

They are two sons of Allenby, the Eccentric, whose story is told on page 23.

David is a senior lecturer at a major university where he is the coordinator of visual arts for the undergraduate program, and head of ceramics within the School of Arts and Education. He leaves shortly for England to finish off a Master of Arts degree in ceramics. His ceramics work is absolutely stunning.

'I purchased my 1972 Ford XY ute in late 1977 after returning from three years in England. On my return, I had a choice of three utes – an XA (which I didn't like because of the large doors) and the pick of two Ford XYs. Being practically minded, I opted for the standard 250 with a bench seat. My brother, Ray, bought the other XY

(a genuine factory 351 with four on the floor, bucket seats and all the other good stuff) some years later.'

Dave is pretty fond of his ute; some 24 years later it is still immaculate. But it nearly wasn't that way. Only a few weeks after David purchased it, he had a night out with Ray. Dave's dry sense of quiet humour becomes highlighted.

'My exuberance in driving home far exceeded the cornering capacity of the ute; survival lead to some pretty severe over-corrections. Testimony to this was the replacement of the rear bearings not too many weeks later. The reality of what could have been led to a new respect for a more sedate driving style when I am in the ute. In fact, anyone coming across me

on the highway would say that the only thing missing is the hat.'

David's faithful friend has travelled far and wide and is in remarkably good condition considering the work it has done.

'It has towed numerous trailer loads of bricks that were used to build a 30 square pottery including several kilns, plus many trailer loads of stone for a large sandstone fence. David is also a great collector of furniture and the ute has always come in handy.

'The ute has been table-drained (like a slippery bog) in central New South Wales, driven through floods between Ivanhoe and Wilcannia, survived severe wind storms camped in a basin in the Grampians and on the foreshore at Ocean Grove.'

The original motor, which has done 260 000 miles, still just keeps ticking over and, according to my mechanic, will do so for many miles yet.'

David does not like lending out the ute, and if he has any brains he won't lend it to that wayward brother of his either!

'Once a lady I was "tracking with" some years back had a spot of car trouble and I lent her my ute to travel back to Melbourne. She rang me to say that she didn't particularly like travelling over 90. (Her car, being more modern, measured in kilometres per hour but my ute speedo shows miles per hour). She had been doing 90 miles an hour, not 90 kilometres an hour. When questioned, she admitted that the trip didn't seem to take her long and that nobody passed her!

'The lady has long since gone and so have a few others, but some things remain constant: I still have my XY ute and it has developed into a long-lasting and trusted friend.'

Blue says, 'I reckon you can put this quote at the start of my story.' (We were having our usual dig at each other. We go at it pretty well, but I still can't get rid of him.)

'Don't you stir me too much,' says Blue 'or I won't come and finish that job.'

'Yeah, that'd be right, ya' mongrel. I've only been waiting nearly a year.'

OK, ya bastard, here's that quote you wanted:

Treasures I have none
Riches I do not crave
Masters I have none
No man calls me slave.

No, Blue didn't write it, but he wishes he had. Sometimes you can't shut him up and other times he just gets obstreperous and it's like pulling teeth trying to get sense out of him. But I wish I had his drive, enthusiasm and talent. He just doesn't know how to stop. He rips what he can from life. He's got more front than a Kenworth truck.

'My first ute was a powder blue EJ Holden. I was at college learning pottery in those days and I had no money, so I just bought any ute that had rego left on it and drove it into the ground. They were all old college dungers — shit heaps! Nearly all Holdens.

'There was a grey EH ute followed by a eucalyptus green FJ, then a cream EH, a pale blue HR, a white HD, a white HT, and a white HG. But then, after college I went into building and I bought an International ute. Then I had a Volkswagon ute that had been a service vehicle for a local VW dealer. I used it to carry stone. Then I bought the 351 XY ute in about 1988. David got his XY in about 1977. I still have it.'

That XY of Blue's has laid idle in the front yard, front wheels missing and slowly decaying, and rust rigor mortis setting in.

'You can say I am restoring it, it's my pride and joy.'

'I'll say that, Blue, when you start work on it. At the moment it's a bloody disgrace and you need to get your act together.'

'Oh yeah, good on ya!'

It's his usual saying – reckon they'll carve it onto his headstone: Here lies Blue – good on ya!

'It's booked into the sheet metal place in a couple of months,' Blue reckons.

'Yeah, yeah, we'll see.' (He's sure he'll get it fully restored.)

Blue has lashed out since he got involved with me and utes. He is beginning to buy more and now has a 1936 Ford side-valve V8 pickup (one of only a few in Australia, he reckons), a Ford twin spinner and he has placed a deposit on a 1956 Ford Mainline ute, and no doubt there'll be more.

In the last book, I mentioned how I got Blue fired up (which is easy) to make his first music CD. Well, the album called *Ute Driving Man* came out some months later under the Bush Larrikin/The Uteman label – 14 original ute driving songs written by Blue, his mate Fred and myself. It's the first homemade Aussie album dedicated to the ute and the people that drive them. Great songs like *Circlework, B&S Ball, Swerve to Miss the Magpies, Working for the Bush,* and other legendary tracks. (It's available from PO Box 46, North Essendon, Vic 3041 $25 plus $3 postage.)

That enough of a 'plug', Blue?

One ute story that Blue tells with his usual laugh-a-minute style was of the FJ ute.

'David and I were on the loose one night and pretty pissed. He was driving. We were heading to a party and came across a swollen creek that had flooded across the road. David said, "What you reckon, Blue?" I replied, "FJs can go anywhere" and so he drove through the water.

'**When the headlights ended up under water we knew we were in the shit. We had to open the doors to stop the ute from floating down the creek. We were too pissed to worry about it, anyway. We survived.**'

I had to ask. I should have known better.

'And what is your final comment about utes, Blue?'

'**It's like a bloke's dick mate – ya just gotta have one.**'

Tania Kernaghan
Cowboy Up to Horsepower

SHE IS USED TO HORSEPOWER, BUT NOW she has a different kind: a bright, new, blue, limited-edition Ford XR8 Pursuit ute – one of the hard-earned rewards for her talent as a multi award-winning country music singer. She has just signed a two-year deal with Ford motor company, who will support her performing work across the country and back her charity work.

Tania Kernaghan is loved across Australia for her singing and her down-to-earth personality. She is a member of one of Australia's foremost families of entertainers. Her brother, Lee Kernaghan, needs no introduction to country music lovers.

Tania calls everyone 'mate' – an example of her relaxed country roots. Her family background can be traced back to the Riverina country near Corowa, New South Wales, where her grandparents were cattle drovers.

Horses and utes have always played a part in the Kernaghan family.

'Dad had a '70s Toyota Hilux ute that he bought to get wood in for our big open fire, and also to go away fishing with, and of course, always to carry horse feed and saddle gear in the back of. **We had horses agisted on the outskirts of Albury, and when I was about eight years old, I remember sitting on Dad's knee in the old ute and steering it as we drove around the horse paddock.'**

'I learnt to ride when I was about four. I used to wake up at 4.30 am and stand by Mum's bed watching her until she woke up, and then we'd be gone and in the saddle by 6.00 am. We would ride and be home by about 10.00 am before the flies were out.'

There was always a keen horse interest in the family – three generations of women in the family would go riding together. Tania and her sister, Fiona, their mother, Pam, and grandmother, Nana Roberts, spent many special times riding together.

'Just as people take their dogs in their utes, we thought nothing of taking our horses in the floats and going off somewhere for a ride. Nana Roberts was a great horsewoman who rode in races during the 1930s. She was a good show jumper too.

She was also the greatest Nana you could ever wish for in your life.

'As a two-year-old, Mum's sister would sit in the saddle in front of Nana and they would jump over obstacles. Mum, her sister and brother all rode horses to school everyday. Mum was also a good influence on all of us to take up riding.

'Nan and Pop Kernaghan were cattle drovers and always on the road. Pop had been in the Australian Light Horse Brigade during World War II. When Dad's brother was born, Pop rode nearly one hundred miles from his camp to see Nan and his new son, and then rode back to his camp the next day.

'When we were growing up, we would often go out to where they were camped with the cattle on reserves and spend the day riding the horses and having a picnic BBQ with them. And when us kids had our own band called Angels & The Blue Devil, we used a horse float to carry Lee's upright piano around.'

Tania has used her fame and appeal to help others and is now patron to the Australian Rodeo Queen competition. She performs regularly at rodeos across Australia and sings the national anthem from the back of a horse.

She is also vice-patron to Princess Anne for the Riding for the Disabled Association and works to raise money for their centres giving talks about the RDA and endorsing their work. The Association has adopted Tania's song *When I Ride* as their theme.

Assisting Tania and Adam Brand to get their sponsorships with Ford was a great thrill for me; they are truly great ambassadors of Australian country music and nicer people you couldn't find. They will both be good for Ford and vice versa. The Kernaghan association with Ford goes back long before Tania, though.

'When Dad was performing years ago, we went around Australia for nine months in 1978 - Dad, Mum, Nana and all us kids in a red Ford GT car, towing a 22-foot caravan. It was so low to the ground with the weight, that when we'd see a road-kill we'd all yell out, "Don't straddle it!" as we knew we'd hit it underneath. Dad used to say how "horny" his GT was and I didn't really understand what he meant until I got the new XR8 ute, and now I really do understand.'

Ray Kernaghan has had a long career in country music and has just released a new album. Some years ago he had a successful song called *Me & Louis on the Road*, a trucking song about a Ford Louisville truck. Ford Motor Company gave Ray one of these trucks to use to promote his song and it was driven all over Australia. Ray also won fame with another Ford truck called 'Waltzing Matilda', the world's first jet powered truck. It was the first truck to exceed 300 kph, and set a world speed record.

Ray also employed a sales rep to sell his records and gave him a Ford Escort panel van for delivering the records to shops. Pam, his wife, later owned a Ford station-wagon. And now Tania carries on the tradition. Tradition runs strong in the Kernaghan family.

'Being involved with Ford is great. I couldn't think of a better company to work with. It is good for country music too! In my V8 Pursuit ute, guys turn their heads; its very cool.'

Tania soon got into song-writing mode with comments like 'Who needs a man when I got a Pursuit ute' or 'When I'm in a ute, I'm always in pursuit'.

Tania's new CD album will be released by the time you read this. I am thrilled to be involved and trust it will be huge for her. She already knows what it is like to have an album 'go platinum' and what it is like to receive many awards too, such as Country Music Association of Australia [CMMA] Female Vocalist of the Year, CMAA Album of the Year Award for *December Moon*, People's Choice Award for Female Vocalist of the Year, CMAA Vocal Collaboration of the Year for *A Bushman Can't Survive*, and many other accolades.

Songs such as *Cowboy Up*, *Boys in Boots*, *Dunroamin' Station*, *True Country*, *Nine Mile Run* and *A Bushman Can't Survive* have all brought a legion of loyal fans for Tania wherever she goes.

Tania is excited about her new album with its new songs like *She'll be Right*, *Going Bush*, *Big Sky Country* and *I Love the Mongrel*. Tania says there are some killer songs on the album, which is being produced by Andrew Farris of super-group, INXS, fame.

'It will be out in November. The musicians are all from the cream of Sydney and Melbourne music – musicians with great talent from the pop industry, and sonically, the album is really fresh and different, but lyrically it is still true country. It is one hundred per cent Australian written, recorded, made and owned.

'Last year I spent a lot of the year on the road touring. I met some terrific people and performed in many towns, and as a result many of the songs reflect those characters and the landscape. With the Year of the Outback in 2002, I will have a year of full-on touring and we'll be going to places all over that we haven't toured before, particularly in the Northern Territory and Western Australia. In Australia we have the best part of the world right in our own backyard.'

The thing that impressed me about Tania and Lee Kernaghan when we met and shared some time, was their great work ethic, and when I mentioned it to their mother she replied, 'They have just worked damned hard.' Something tells me they had good inspiration and backing from their parents. Their professionalism always shines through.

Readers may see Tania riding around in her beloved ute.

A couple of days after she got the XR8 in Tamworth, I rang her on the mobile to catch up with her; she was in a carwash.

She later went out to a rodeo to show all the boys. Tania loves her XR8 and is happy to show it off to her fans. If you don't find her driving the XR8, her future plans with horses may give an indication as to where you'll find her when she's not on stage performing.

'I'd love to spend time riding the High Country. I love camping out with horses. As a kid I enjoyed pony club and gymkhanas. Now I'm really keen to become more involved in competing with cutting horses. I've always wanted to own a quarter horse. That is my aim now.'

Whether it is horse riding or touring and singing for her fans, you can be sure Tania will always give it her best. Nothing less than one hundred per cent is the Kernaghan way.

If you feel a bit 'down' you just have to spend five minutes with Tania Kernaghan and you'll feel like a million dollars. She has an infectious love of life that rubs off. No wonder people love her.

Onya, TK – you're a bloody legend – mate.

You can catch up with all the latest on Tania at - *taniakernaghan.com.au*

The Ute

It doesn't matter what make or model, but it must be a ute.

Some would go for an Adler
  - if they could find one
or an Armstrong Siddeley,
  or an Austin - that's cute
A Bedford, Commer, Chrysler and Chev.
  A Datsun, a Dodge
an Exide, Federal or Ford
  Australian Ford, English Ford
and American Ford
  a Fargo and a Graham, if found
What about a Hillman, Holden, Hudson
  International, perhaps?
J is for Jeep, a Lawton is rare
  But there's Mercedes, Morris and Nissan,
Reo, Reville, Rover, Rugby

A Standard is a Vanguard,
Subaru and Suzuki
  Ta-Ta from India
or a Toyota from Japan
  A Vauxhall or a Willys
If they aren't for you, do not despair
  There's even a Z
And ...
  Z is for a Zeta
Maybe you'll buy one,
  But I don't know where.

And so you've finally chosen a make, but what model?

An XY, XT, XA, AB or XC
  maybe an FX, FJ, EH or EJ,
A VS, a VT or VU or an XR is beaut
  A flat-top, styleside, well-type,
a coupe, one-tonner,
  trayback, deep-well or other?

Four wheel, six wheel
  or even a three wheel?
Four or six cylinders, or a big V8,
  And even V10 or 12?

Automatic, trimatic,
  three on the tree,
pushbutton or not
  four, five and now six on the floor,
air-con, recon, electric or wind.

Two wheel drive, four wheel drive
  or all wheel drive.
LSD, cruise control,
  push button this
and push button that.
  AM/FM, wireless, radio,
digital or TV or CD – digital or not.
  Remote this and remote that.
Laser beam out of sight,
  gizmos that shine in the night
Inclinometer, GPS or trip tracker.
  Compact disc, single or stacker,
Mirrors that move and cut out the light,
  windows tinted to a shade of the
night,

Me, I don't care – I just want a ute.

Life is a hoot when you own a ute!

The Pride & Joy

'It took me a bit to get it to the way I wanted it; a bit of paint, custom interior with SAAS seats, motor enhancements and a few thousand dollars worth of stereo. The 308 V8 motor is running four volt mains, Chevy internals, custom spec row cam, L34 heads, roller rockers and low compression pistons for the future dream of super-charging it. It has a 15-inch B45 Simmons house, 265 tyres and a bolt LSD diff to turn them. To finish it off, a bit of

'FOR ME TO SELL AN HSV SS COMMODORE in order to buy another, the new one had to be something that I thought was pretty good. It didn't take much convincing for me to do it so that I could buy my pride and joy - a 1976 HJ one-tonner - off one of my friends.

'Once it was my daily-driven work-horse but nowadays it only gets pulled out of the shed when I want to go for a drive - just the way I like it.

marine carpet on the back tray for the dog to wipe his feet – and Kylie too, ha ha!'

Greg Jerrett is 25 and knows how to appreciate life. A spare parts manager with Rod Dugan Ford in Gunnedah, he lives on 18 acres out from Boggabri with Kylie, who is a photographer, and Bronson, the four-year-old Rottweiler.

He has had a bad 12 months, however.

'The ute has laid dormant for about a year as I have been trying to fight off cancer. I have had three major operations to try and get rid of it and although the operations were successful at the time, the cancer grew back very aggressively to the stage where it was inoperable. I am the first person in Australia to take part in a clinical trial of a new chemo-type tablet, and the latest news after a few months of being on the tablet is that the cancer is in remission. At the moment it looks good but only time can tell the eventual outcome.

'For the time being, I am still not able to do much work on the one-tonner, but it won't be long until I'll be back out in the shed planning what to do with it next. Although, the longer I look at it, the more I want to do to it.

'I know they say that beating cancer has a lot to do with having a positive attitude, and it does, but it also helps to have goals and one of them for me is to have a tonner that looks good with great performance.'

Well, the country folk of Australia know how to look after their own. Greg has had to be in Adelaide and Sydney for tests and operations. All very expensive but people rallied. His employer has been tremendous. Greg will have his job to return to and when they were in Adelaide, Stillwell Ford gave Greg and Kylie an AU Ford for driving around and for getting to hospital for tests.

The town of Boggabri decided they needed to help this great young bloke. The Boggy Beaut Ute Show was put on in aid of Greg. Twenty-eight utes turned up from Tamworth, Narrabri, Gunnedah and as far away as Dubbo. Numerous suppliers donated great prizes.

'It was a great family day. There was a heap of things for the kids, not just for ute drivers – tug-o-war, jump castle, three-legged races, all sorts of stuff. A few hundred people turned up throughout the day and the event raised over $4000 towards the medical bills.

'It was really overwhelming. I can't believe the amount of support and the lengths they went to. The town is now saying they hope to make it an annual event for others who need help. As one person said, it brought a lot of people together who normally might not get together. It was an atmosphere of people helping people and that is so important in a small community.'

How would he describe it in a few words? 'It was bloody unbelievable!'

Greg's case brought wide media attention. He was interviewed by nine newspapers, did 10 radio interviews and appeared on national television on Today Tonight. It highlighted the support Greg has in his country friends – the country at work.

While the day took it out of Greg a bit, it gave him a new lease of life. He tells me that this morning he took the ute for a drive into town.

'I even put a new battery in her as I couldn't jump-start her all the time. It was great to drive her again.'

We trust you will drive her for many, many years yet, mate.

'Tassie'

'He's a skinny-ribbed, ferret-headed, big-eared, big-nosed bloody Tasmanian.'

WELL, PETER 'TASSIE' CAMPBELL DOESN'T need enemies when he's got mates like local mechanic, Warwick 'Mongrel' Gregory.

When I finally got Tas on his own to interview him, what did he say? 'They give me a heap of shit, but I give them plenty in return.

'They even buy me an extra pot of beer, which is for me two heads, they reckon. The reason why us Tasmanians have two heads is because when we come over here, the Victorian heads are no bloody good, so we gotta bring an extra one for them.'

There's a mutual admiration society in Murchison, Victoria, well known for its characters and ute drivers. The centre of gossip, fun and frivolous entertainment for the boys is the garage that I nicknamed 'Mongrel Motors' - it featured in both *Beaut Utes* and the sequel, *More Beaut Utes*. Now it is Tassie's turn to hold up the tradition for Murch.

'Tas turned up here out of the blue and we haven't been able to get rid of the bastard ever since. We've tried, he takes a lot of shit, but he gives a lot as well,' says Mongrel with a huge belly laugh.

Tas says, 'I'll still be around for a while yet; they can't get rid of me that easy. I am thinking of taking up karate or doing a body-building course and then a few more might get thrown out of the pub in the near future.'

Tassie is referring to the day when all the locals were enjoying some chiacking at his expense in the local pub.

'Some vintage cars pulled up and when the owners walked in, Burkie says in a loud voice, "Go on Tassie, tell them now what a heap of shit their cars are". I

nearly died. Anyway, everyone is having a laugh and when Burkie gets up to leave he picks me up by the shirt collar and carries me outside. He's about 17 stone and about six foot four. I'm five foot nine and nearly nine stone fully dressed with my pockets full of lead. Anyway, I walked back in and

said, "Well, I sure got rid of him". It cracked them up! Imagine me even trying to lift him.'

Underneath all the fun and games there is a genuine respect for Tas and vice versa. Mongrel says, 'He fitted in really well with the locals right off and he's always been a worker, I'll give him that. He's a true Aussie, a good bloke.'

When I questioned Tas he said, 'I love Murch, it's a terrific place. You know what they're like.' (I do. I agree. They are a pack of bastards, Tas).

'I have been known to have a light drink on a warm day, but you can't help the company you have to put up with, though. No really, I'll be staying here, a great place and good people, I don't think I'll ever leave.'

When he worked at a chook farm they called him 'Feathers' but 'Tassie' is what they all know him as, mainly.

'Many people here in town wouldn't even know my real name; everyone just calls me Tas or Tassie and that's OK.'

Peter 'Tas' Campbell was born in Queenstown, Tasmania. His father worked at the Mt Lyell mine as an oil store attendant. Tas started his apprenticeship as an electrician in 1961. He worked at the Mt Lyell mine until 1984. His son, Brent, still lives there and works as a mill operator/labourer at the same mine his father and grandfather both worked.

Tas worked for a local earth-moving machinery company as a truck driver for a number of years before moving to Murchison, Victoria in 1991 and has been there ever since. (His wife, Wendy, had a cousin who owned the local caravan park.) Since then Tas has done general farm work, maintenance and management work on a chicken farm for three years and now says he is a weedkiller. Actually, he works for a local company spraying crops and roadsides. He sprays by hand, from a motorbike or from a vehicle, mainly a Toyota Landcruiser with a boom spray. He works locally or in the north or northeast of the Goulburn Valley.

Peter and Wendy have been married for 31 years and their daughter, Fiona, also lives in Murchison with her son, Jacob Peter. He is three and, you can tell, is adored by Tassie.

And what about the mighty Tas ute?

'That's "Bluey the Beaut Ute". He's a 1976 Datsun 1500. I saw it on the side of the road near Goornong with a 'For Sale- $600' sign on it. I came back and told Mongrel about it and he said it sounded good, so I offered the bloke $500. Mongrel Motors put in a new clutch and windscreen

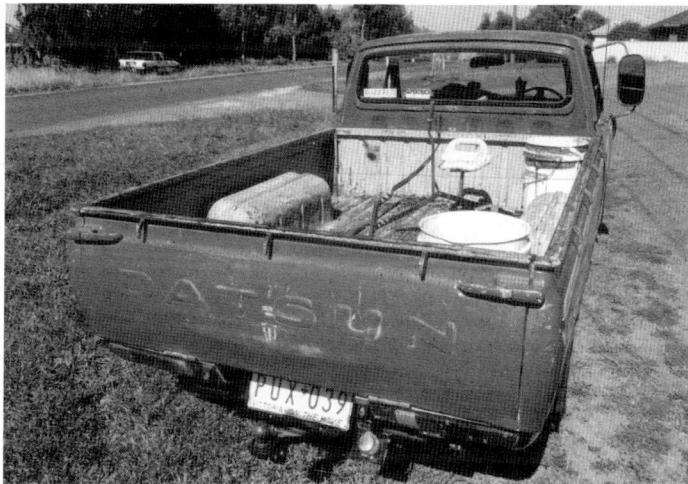

and a couple of tyres. She's been going three years.

Tas can't go anywhere without his grandson, Jacob and Bluey the Beaut Ute.

'It's a general get-around ute. It carts stuff to the tip and wood for my daughter's fires. I've shifted her in it twice. We never lock it up here. It's got a big toolbox bolted on the back. Everyone throws their cans in the back of it. I washed it about a month ago. She's just an everyday, bloody good vehicle. Ideal for what I want. She's a bloody good ute, she's a little pearler, Bluey the Beaut Ute. Even my three year old grandson, Jacob, can say "Bluey the Beaut Ute".'

Do Mongrel Motors look after it? 'Well, between them and me she's gonna be doing a few miles yet.'

The day he turned up to have his photo taken at Mongrel Motors, he had a half-flat tyre and so he delayed the film shoot, but we waited.

'**Mind you, when you go into Mongrel Motors, you want a good job, so you do most of the work yourself. I call it the "Beehive" - they sure know how to sting!**'

Well, Tassie, I reckon you owe me a beer seeing as I stuck up for you; and I'm not too proud to drink that one for your second head. Make it a large one, mate.'

The Legend

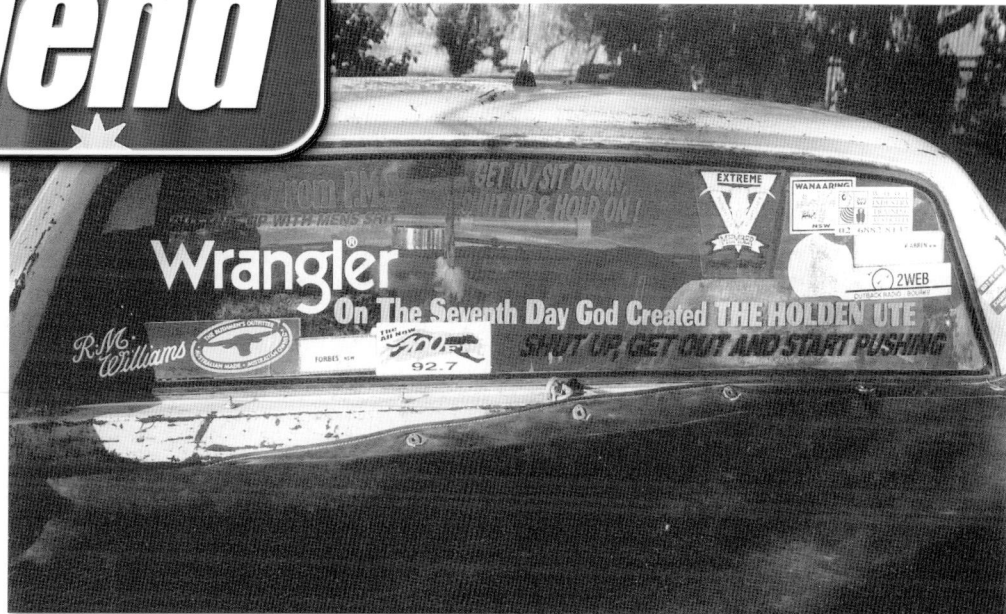

SHE'S GOT THAT TRUE-BLUE, DINKY-DI, down-to-earth bushie spirit. She's independent and strong-willed. She's a mum. She works hard but knows how to cry when she has to. When you get to know her, you feel that she can take on just about anything and will come through it. But she has her moments and we've talked about the good and the bad things of life. She's done it tough at times.

Don't ask her about banks, though!

One day she'll have a good yarn to tell her grandkids about a bank and a ute-load of sheep; but for legal reasons she cannot reveal full details here. Let's just say she got the bank to take notice.

It was a final protest about a major stuff-up that had put getting her own farm in jeopardy. She had felt like dumping a load of sheep manure on the front doorstep of the bank but knew she'd have to pay to clean it up. But there's always more than one way to win. How many Australians would just love to make a stand and take on the banks? She did and won.

Judy Mitchell has the get-up-and-go to do anything. Her ute is called 'Jessie May the Legend', but I reckon Jude herself may be the legend.

'Jess is no flash ute, but I love her to death. I'm a shearer's cook, rouseabout, penner-upper, presser, fencer, cattle worker and master of nothing in particular. But I have a go and my Jess is right up there with me. **She's an HX that's been from one end of Aussie to the other. She's been stolen twice; I got her back a little worse for wear, but I'll never let her go. She's got a history that never ends.'**

Jude gets almost as excited about utes as I do and we spent hours talking about them. Her life could fill a book very easily and she's only 36.

She has worked all over Australia. I knocked up nine pages when interviewing her and that was just about the jobs she'd had and the towns she'd worked in.

'The first real trip the ute went on was when I woke up in my ute after a hard night. My boyfriend and his mate decided to hijack me and the ute and take us with them to Kangaroo Island for a couple of months.

'Since then the ute and I have worked in places in New South Wales like Lightning Ridge, White Cliffs, Tilpa, Louth, Wanaaring, Wilcannia, Carinda, Quambone, Brewarrina, Godooga, Angledool, Hebel, Job's Gate, Barringun, Enngonia and Hay. Then in Queensland I've worked at Toompine, Thargomindah, Quilpie,

Charleville, Aromanga, Isisford, Blackall, Longreach.

'I've worked in both the Simpson and the Great Sandy Deserts (our camp moved from Port Fairy in Victoria to the Charleville region in Queensland, up through Three Ways, Camooweal, Turkey Creek and Halls Creek to Great Sandy in from Sandfire in Western Australia). And in Western Australia it was places like the Hamersley Ranges, Wittenoom and beyond, the Kimberleys, Marble Bar, Newman, Jigalong Mission and many more.

'I'd have to get the diaries out, but these are a few of the places that I've worked. Did I tell you I stowed away on a ship and two weeks later ended up in Japan for two days and then spent another two weeks coming home?'

And what sorts of jobs has Jude done in these places? Well, she has retired from the shearing industry five times but is back in it yet again. She is completing her wool-classing certificate at the moment. Other than that she has worked as a labourer, barmaid, cleaning contractor, jillaroo, side-show alley operator (making fairy floss), canteen operator, tea lady, singer (of jingles on radio and at a bowls club), electrical assistant (first woman in the electrical department of Mount Newman mines), waitress and cook (at a hotel in Port Hedland which is in the record books as having had the most stabbings in one night), hairdresser, jelly wrestler, odd jobs person, sidecar racer (with the Beagle Boys), tractor driver (on cotton farms), cotton ginner, lawn mower, dress shop sales assistant, café owner, fencing contractor (doing big government jobs in Western Australia), and caterer (caramel slices and biscuits). Jude has also worked on seismic oil exploration crews. Since 1992 she has mended shearing pants under her business name of 'Dungaree Doctor'. She also sells wool products and does oil paintings.

'A typical day for me can start from 4.30 am and I work until between 10.00 pm and midnight. A 'sleep-in' for me is 6.00 am.

My grandmother (I model my life on her) was one hell of a woman, just absolutely amazing and she always said, "Take every opportunity that comes your way and never let a chance go by you."

'Mum was pretty amazing too; she brought up three kids on her own and she was a big influence also. But I spent a lot of time with my grandmother in my young years.'

Jude is a mum too. Her son, Shaun, is her greatest off-sider and he loves 'their truck'.

Jude finally has her own farm now. She has put down some roots and plans to make it the best farm she can. She grew up on the land; her grandmother owned a large property. 'This is it, I ain't going anywhere – well, at least for 10 years, anyway.'

And so it came to an end. How was I going to finish this story about this amazing woman? I needed her final thoughts about utes.

'It's hard to explain, but when I get behind the wheel of the ute, there's something about it. I get that warm, fuzzy feeling all over. I can't help but look at other utes; they are different somehow – friendly.

'A ute just makes me feel good, right to the core.'

Toyota Tonka!

He turned 18 about seven weeks ago. He bought it about six weeks ago.

I WAS HEADED HOME, SO WAS HE - IN THE opposite direction. His bright yellow ute was almost the same colour as mine. We could see each other coming in the heavy traffic. He flashed his lights and I gave him a wave. Will I or won't I? Yeah, why not.

By the time I managed to make a U-turn in the traffic, he was long gone. I drove back about 15 kilometres but he had turned off into a local town. I went past and then decided to turn off and take another road back through the town just in case. Sure enough, he was coming on the road towards me again. We both flashed our lights and pulled over.

'I thought I was seeing my twin brother ute,' he laughed as he got out. He had a mate with him and another pulled up in a car as well. I took some photos in between dodging the traffic. He was headed bush to do a bit of off-roading so we swapped addresses and phone numbers and I caught up with him later. Gerald Edmonds has always liked four-wheel drives.

'I was looking for a four-wheel drive and a mate said there was one for sale just around the corner. I went and saw it and thought it was awesome. I bought it for about $6500 and all I've done to it is get a sign-writer bloke to make the sticker on the tailgate. It cost me $20. When I first saw it I thought it looked like a Tonka toy - and big boys have big toys.'

Gerald was born and bred in the bush. His father has just traded in his 1999 Holden Rodeo ute for a twin cab Toyota Hilux. Dad owns a shed construction business and the family also owns a farm out of town that grows oats, cattle and sheep. Gerald has started a four-year carpentry apprenticeship in the family business and two teams of two work all over erecting sheds, garages, tanks, gates, cubbies - whatever you want. Gerald really likes being in the building game.

His siblings are Sandy, Harvey, Cameron, Luke and Trudy. Surprisingly for a family with property, they have no dogs. Gerald learnt to drive when he was about six or seven and had a Morris Minor 1000 as a paddock bomb when he was about eleven.

Later the paddock bomb was a $50 Renault. Country kids learn young.

'It's a pretty standard ute. The bloke I got it off was about 20. He bought it as a wreck and did it up as a project. It's got a bullbar, a rollbar and spotlights. I've also got some side steps that I might put on. I won't do anything to it until I've paid it off, though. It has had a few little electrical faults to fix; other than that it hasn't missed a beat.'

Gerald has already taken the Tonka to the mountains for some off-road experience. He seems excited by the thrill of adventure. He is young and energetic and one who is going to see a lot of the bush, I think. Only time will tell.

One thing is for sure; he has a bright coloured ute and you can see him coming for miles. I like his taste in colours. If you see it, give the Toyota Tonka a wave.

Ute musters

WA 'Dessy' WOWSERS

Dessy spent his school years living in railway camps on the trans-Australia line, east of Kalgoorlie. Then he worked in a few mines for a bit before studying mining engineering.

'I was assaulted in the street one night and received bad head injuries; nearly went blind and suffered memory problems. I dropped out of uni and had a tough, depressed couple of years.

'I managed to lob a good job in '94 logging drill holes for the exploration industry. **I became involved in directional drilling and spent two of the greatest years of my life living in mining camps and sleeping in swags anywhere between Marvel Loch, Magnet, Cue, Wiluna, Jundee, Bronzewing, Laverton**

'WE'VE PRETTY WELL ALWAYS HAD UTES in the family. I think the first I ever drove was the FB - sitting on my Dad's knee steering around the backyard. Grandfather had it from new and when he died in the 1970s it was left to Dad. The old grey pulled some heavy loads for about the next 15 years, eventually the radiator kept dying so the old duck got retired to the back shed. The old man has threatened to sell it a couple of times, but that's the next project: to get it back on the road. We'll keep it original, it's a beauty.'

For some unexplained reason, David Aitken has been known as 'Des' since he was 14 and is now nicknamed 'Dessy'. He reckons he is 30 going on 19. His ute is a yellow '82 WB 253.

and as far as Karonie. I went back to study part-time but ran out of money and worked directional drilling again for a year.'

Dessy was approached by a mining company about 18 months ago to work in his current role as open pit supervisor. He also plans to return to some part-time study.

'I love life, my ute, Emu Bitter, Bundy, my RM boots and women. Oh, and the dog, Helmut. One of my pet hates is people who indicate too late when driving.'

One unusual story Dessy relates is of the time he 'found out that the "nice" Japanese people that I used to meet weekly on Banjawarn Station between

Leinster and Laverton (and who mysteriously disappeared in 1995) were actually using the brand new shearing shed to test their sarin gas on the livestock before a planned release in the Tokyo subways.'

Dessy is a member of the Kalgoorlie AAWP, a political group whose initials stand for Australians Against Wowsers Party. Some of their policies include such issues as beer, pies, BBQs and 'corporal punishment for the fun police'. Their tongue-in-cheek fight is against wowsers, political correctness, beer taxes and tofu and lentil burgers.

'The AAWP was born out of our frustration with the WA government's

decision to ban riding in the back of utes and a few other things. We had a bloke run for the seat of Kalgoorlie and he got about five per cent of the vote – not bad for a zero-budget campaign. We made a bit of noise and had a ball.'

Dessy has spent a lot of time in the remote Western Australian bush travelling, over the years, many thousands of kilometres to work sites.

'You learn a few things out there – respect for the bush. Never take it for granted. Always take water, always have a map and always let someone know where you are.

'I never get sick of driving. How could you? The bush is so beautiful.'

WB

attends Glenormiston Agricultural College where he learns all about ground preparation, plant make-up, nutrients and more.

The ute is not a farm ute as such. The tractors and trailer take care of the vegetables.

'Dad bought the ute from a caryard about four years ago and I've had it now for about two years. He takes it when he wants it. It's had a few motors and gearboxes - we've rebuilt the 5-litre 308 twice. It has a CB and radio, bullbar and spotlights. I'd like to add a rollbar, extractors and twin exhaust system.'

I asked why he likes utes.

'I live in the country; they look better and go harder. Dad has always had one-tonners, mainly Holden HQs.'

Ian and Kay Peelman have a 16-year-old daughter, Casey, as well as a son who intends to continue carrying on the family tradition of growing vegetables. Utes are a family tradition now too. As Ben says:

'There's always been a ute lying around the house.'

HE WAS OUT CRUISING IN THE UTE WITH a mate and two others in another ute. They spotted my ute parked on the side of the road, so they stopped to have a yarn and check out my vehicle. They already had copies of my earlier ute books and were pretty keen to be in this one, so it was photo time there and then.

Ben Peelman is a fourth generation farmer. His great-grandfather bought a dairy farm that was later converted to a vegetable farm. Ben's grandfather and father both worked the property. Ben's father, Ian, is now a concrete truck driver and Ben grows vegetables fulltime.

At the moment he grows about ten acres with a weekly pick of about five bins of spinach, five bins of silverbeet and two bins of endive. Ben takes his truckload to the city market and sells through an agent.

Now into the second year of a three-year apprenticeship as a vegetable grower, Ben

Wrecks & Relics

and moved to the city where getting about was easier on public transport. He repaired buses for two years until he was retrenched.

It was then he realised he needed to get some education to ensure he would not be retrenched as easily. So he went back to school and got an Associate Diploma in Refrigeration and Air Conditioning. He then went on to do an apprenticeship as a plumber, eventually becoming a master plumber and gasfitter.

He now works on commercial and industrial sites – mainly shopping centres, hospitals, large apartment blocks, showgrounds and the like. His fiancée, Sue, is a city girl who works for Myers and she is also a qualified teacher. She's not into utes. Dean reckons he'll probably have to stay in the city.

'I've owned the HZ since I was about 17. One of the caryards in Clare brought it into the panel beaters where I was employed as an apprentice for some work. The boss was going to buy it but he didn't so I bought it for $4000. They had $6500 on it if it went to the yard. Dad paid for it and I paid him back.

Yellow 'HZ'

BEING BORN ON A FARM IN SOUTH Australia's north, Dean Lewcock was always around utes. He works in Adelaide now but longs to go back to the bush. He gets back to the farm as often as possible. It is a mixed farm with sheep, vineyards and some hay.

Dean left school and did an apprenticeship as a panel beater but lost his licence

'I was going to do it up when I had an accident in it. It has a 202 with column auto and a bench seat that I kept in case I ever had company. It is yellow and as stock standard as ever.

'All I did to her for the first couple of years was to add extractors, a two-inch exhaust system, larger V8 radiator, air horn, four lights, UHF, spotlights, bullbar, centre aerial, and mag wheels. The "Old Girl" has been over most of South Australia plus to a couple of B&S Balls when I was younger and single.

'**It has never been kept undercover. It has only broken down a couple of times. I've always tried to keep it mechanically good even if the body has been neglected. It has towed everything from car trailers with my FX car on it, to tandem tipper, to all sorts of farm implements.**'

Dean rattles off just a few of the things it has carried over the years including his twenty-first birthday beer keg, furniture of various shapes and sizes, firewood, car parts from complete motors to spares, farm animals (mainly sheep and dogs), friends' dogs, motorbikes, work-tools for plumbing, and humans of both sexes. He has slept in the back of it numerous times with and without company.

'**"The Old Girl" as I call it, is often known by other people as the "Yellow Terror", "Yellow Banana", "Yellow Submarine" or "Yellow Bus".** When I lost my licence for eleven months when I was about 22, I kept it on the farm and the family used it.'

Dean has spent many years working at restoring his FX sedan but his affection for his ute is evident.

'The Old Girl has been good to me over the years. I don't know why I've kept it so long. I'm now 34 and I guess it's been a necessity as I've changed jobs, moved accommodation, studied full-time – it's been handy, been there and never cost much to keep going.'

The Lewcock family have all known their share of utes. Dean's father has had a Hillman Commer ute, an HK, an HJ (which Dean now has also), and a Mazda Bravo. Dean's brother, Glenn, has had a Datsun 4WD tray top, and then a 1995 Holden twin cab with canopy. Other brother, Kym, has had a WB Holden, which has since been sold to buy a 4WD.

Finally, of utes Dean says, 'They are just part and parcel of country life.'

'You never know unless you have a go'

The Bumper Man

HE WAS FILLING UP WITH PETROL AT A BP service station as I went past. Naturally, I hit the brakes and drove back to check out what all the car parts were.

'G'day, mate, you got a bit of a load on there,' says I.

From there it didn't take me long to explain why I was interested in his load. We both had hundred of kilometres to go and in opposite directions, so we swapped business cards. I took a photo and let him hit the road. He'd been to Deniliquin,

Finley and district and was headed south. I was headed north, then east towards Sydney.

Grant Cowell's father, Cliff, owned a panel beating shop for 30 years. He is retired now and living near the lakes. Grant grew up spending his after-school hours in the shop where he learnt what panel beating was all about.

For the past 12 years Grant has managed one of the largest plastic repair shops. When he started, he and three blokes repaired about 10 to 12 bars a day. Twelve years later there was a total staff of 24 repairing over 100 bars a day.

'After all that time they shafted me, so I left to start my own business,' says Grant.

With years of experience and a large number of contacts in the industry all over the country, Grant should do well. He has a heap of people who want to work for him, so that is a good start – but not just yet. 'I'm starting off small and will slowly build it. I am in the process of getting agents to find me a factory.'

There are 290 bumpers in the backyard at the moment waiting to go into the factory and hundreds more on the way. Grant was leaving the day after I interviewed him for another trip to far-east Gippsland, and then back to New South Wales again for another load.

'In the bush there are not many plastic repairers and so most panel shops just throw damaged bumpers in the backyard and get a deal with other suppliers. I have a huge number of contacts, so I will be repairing plastic bumpers and selling them back to the trade cheaper than buying a new part. I'll be selling genuine and non-genuine parts and I'll also have access to almost any other part a person wants, if it's not in stock. The name of my business will be "Bayside Bumpers".

'I do all sorts of plastic welding which is a bit of a specialist field. Most of the bumpers I recondition are for late model vehicles from 1990s on – Ford, Holden, Mitsubishi, Toyota, Honda. I do, however, have a lot of parts from earlier XF Fords onwards and Holdens from VN on. I also do just about any form of plastic welding for motorbikes, flaring around headlights, whatever.

'Plastic welding is just like panel beating without the hammer. It is hard to get the experience and you need to know plastics. The majority of the work is done with heat. A special plastic welder costs about $800 and the rest of the tools are like the normal hand tools you see in a panel shop.'

Grant's ute is a standard 1996 Holden Rodeo with a 2.7 litre motor, 5-speed, with duel fuel. He has just bought it and with 160 000 kilometres on the clock, he will soon knock up some miles. Grant tows a trailer all the time when collecting his parts, and when I saw him he said it was not a very big load. He often tows a bigger trailer that is loaded over the roof. At one time he was going to buy a van but soon realised the ute was the way to go - he can load it up with a lot more bumper parts.

This story highlights how important a ute can be to a person. 'The ute is basically my livelihood; couldn't live without it for collecting and doing deliveries,' says Grant.

'Without it I'd be stuffed.'

Acknowledgements

Special thanks to Geoff Hocking, graphic designer and Karen Masman, editor, who with me, make up the 'A-Team' – thanks guys for the usual great job.

Many thanks to Ali Watts, Managing Editor, who, sadly, has now left Penguin, but was tops throughout the two projects we worked on together. (We love her still even though she barracks for Essendon.)

Thanks to Clare Forster, publisher, who always believed in the ongoing projects. Many more hopefully, Clare.

Also thanks to Tony Palmer, Design Studio at Penguin, and Anne Rogan, Managing Editor, Penguin.

To my Agent, Debbie Golvan, who always works in my best interests, and Colin Golvan for his added legal support.

Kevin Masman (computer files transfers).

John & Sue Butler (letter re Tony Berry's A-Model).

Colin Barr, Digitype (cover photo).

Haylee Bradley (cover model).

Ray Stevens (Dodge ute on cover).

The photos were taken by the author using an old 1975 Canon FT 35mm with wide angle lens, Kodak Gold 100 film stock and using natural light only.

Thanks to those who helped with photos not taken by The Uteman, due to time constraints that made it impossible to travel interstate at the last minute. They include:

Norval McClean, photographer, Emu Plains NSW (Adam Brand [except p17] and Tania Kernaghan).

David Landua, photographer, Dubbo, NSW (Judy Mitchell's story).

Andrew Whitttacker, NSW (Boggy Ute Show).

General Motors Holden and Ford Australia for ute photos.

Special thanks to anyone who I may have forgotten to acknowledge; many thanks to everyone for interest and support.

Thanks to the regular supporters of The Uteman website (uteman.com.au) who have always offered suggestions and shown great support for the site and shared their love of their utes. Great Australians. Thanks to major sponsors, Ford Australia, who have shown fantastic support for some years now and it continues.

Particular mention to Kevin 'Henry' Lillie, Jason Miller, Brett Hewitt, Deb Chan, Beth Ward, Geoff Ulm, and finally engineer Mike ('It's Beer o'clock') Duthie who is also known to often mutter, 'You can't do that!' Thanks also to his engineering mate, Russell Burns ('That's not quite right!') and the other stalwarts in the Ford Corner at the 'Hotham' in Geelong. A great bunch who provide services and ongoing support for The Uteman 'Working for the Bush' campaign.

To all the special people who have their stories here, my greatest thanks for your time and generosity in sharing your lives with me and the readers.

To all ute drivers across Australia, travel safe and - Keep on Uteing!

The Author

ALLAN M. NIXON is a full-time freelance writer and journalist, who writes the *'Beaut Utes'* feature column for R. M. Williams *OUTBACK* magazine. *Beaut Utes 3* is his fifteenth published book.

Since the original *Beaut Utes* book became a bestseller in 1998, he has travelled all over Australia, judging ute shows, searching for special stories and collecting utes. He has judged shows as far away as south of Perth in Western Australia, to far north Queensland, and many in Victoria and New South Wales. *More Beaut Utes* became a bestseller in 2000.

In 1998 he completed a Melbourne-Perth-Melbourne return trip with six utes, raising money for his favourite charities, Royal Flying Doctor Service, and REACHOUT!, a youth suicide prevention charity.

In recognition of his work, Ford Motor Company offered to sponsor him in his endeavours and assist him to travel Australia by providing an XR8 ute. His association with Ford has resulted in a 'Beaut Utes' raffle of an XR8 ute, raising money for kids with cancer in conjunction with the Apex Foundation. It is planned that this raffle will be an annual one.

The ongoing relationship with Ford has resulted in Allan's building of 'The Mongrel' ute and a wide range of activities across Australia. He was also intrumental in Adam Brand's and Tania Kernaghan's gaining of a sponsorship with Ford.

He released a *Beaut Utes 2000 Calendar*, and *Beaut Utes 3* is the latest in an ongoing series. There are two other ute books in development at the moment.

He was the instigator of a CD called *Ute Drivin' Man*, the first music CD of 14 original songs totally dedicated to the ute, recorded in partnership with Ray Stuchbery on the Bush Larrikin/The Uteman label.

Australia's original website devoted to the ute, *The Uteman* (uteman.com.au) started in 1998, attracts a huge following.

Allan 'The Uteman' Nixon lives at the base of a mountain range north of Melbourne, with his wife, Janette, two dogs, Rowdy and Lady, two chooks, six magpies and an abundance of wildlife.

Books by Allan M. Nixon

Beaut Utes 3
Jokes for Blokes
More Beaut Utes
Real Men Talking
Beaut Utes 2000 Calendar
Beaut Utes
Humping Bluey: Swagmen of Australia
Pocket Positives: A-Z of Inspirational Quotations
Stand & Deliver: 100 Australian Bushrangers
Somewhere in France: Sgt Roy Whitelaw, WW1, 1914-1918
The Grinham Report: A Family History
100 Australian Bushrangers: 1789-1901
Inglewood Gold: 1859-1901
Muddy Boots: Inglewood Football Club
Inglewood: Gold Town of Early Victoria